JOURNEYS WITHIN

JOURNEYS WITHIN
Sourcebook of Guided Meditations

LISA DAVIS

FINDHORN
Press

Text © Lisa Davis 1995
First published 1995

ISBN 1 899171 35 5

British Library Cataloguing-in-Publication Data
A catalogue record for this book is available from the British Library.

Set in ITC New Baskerville and Eras
Cover illustration © Harley Miller 1995
Cover Design by Patricia Andersson
Printed and bound by WSOY, Finland

Published by
Findhorn Press
The Park, Findhorn,
Forres IV36 0TZ, Scotland
01309-690582/ fax 690036
e-mail thierry@findhorn.org

CONTENTS

For Jools and Cruella de Ville, who taught me how to give and receive unconditional love

Acknowledgements:
To Irene Reddish, my sister-friend, many, many 'thank you's' for your constant support, encouragement and love for over twenty years
To Paul Johnston, my computer guru, thank you for always being there when I need you
To Jane McDermott for sacred sound, and especially thank you for lovely food and laughter
To Chris Sell and Laran, for their wisdom and the purity of their teaching
To Eileen Baldwin, Doreen Nicholson, Elaine Sauvé, David Edwards, Brian Thirlwell, and to everyone in the Monday night and Friday night groups, my thanks for all the love and laughter
To Julie Soskin for your wisdom, and for creating a safe, sacred space which gave me the courage I needed
To Judy Hall for your encouragement and for allowing me to use the meditation I learned from you
To Jools, Lucy, Chloe and William for keyboard and filing assistance (whether I needed it or not !) love and purrs
To Thierry and Karin Bogliolo at Findhorn Press for bringing out this book so joyfully and gracefully
And, finally, my love and gratitude to Irjana of the seventh layer of the spiral of light

INTRODUCTION

I can recall the time, back in the 1960s, when the New Age was surrounded in mystery and hovering on the far-distant horizon. Tarot cards were unavailable in the United Kingdom and anyone interested in spiritual development was labelled a crank or (even worse at that time) a witch.

Fortunately public awareness has expanded and the tools for self-growth are now available to everyone. Tarot cards, crystals, astrological readings and spiritual healing are readily available from a number of sources. Alternative therapies such as homeopathy, aromatherapy and shiatzu are now clearly acknowledged by the health-care establishment and, in some areas, are funded through the National Health Service. More and more and more the concepts of self-healing and personal growth are being recognised and validated. At long last the cranky things I have been involved with since childhood have gained general acceptance. My work with tarot, sound, crystals and healing energy no longer causes people to raise their eyebrows and take a step backwards.

Whilst working both with others seeking healing and relief from stress and anxiety and attempting to deal with the many challenges within my own life, I have found guided meditation to be one of the most useful and powerful tools for self-healing, personal growth and transformation. Inner journeys, as they are sometimes called, have brought a richness to my daily living, a deep understanding and awareness of my self, and they have allowed me to over-come seemingly insurmountable obstacles, heal relation-ships, access my creativity and, on a more mundane level, manage the stresses of life and personal illness.

In these uncertain times more and more people are seeking a new path. A way of living and being which will enable them to access their own power and help them on their journey towards increased awareness and spirituality. Guided meditations can be used for mental, emotional and physical self-healing, to heal others, develop intuition and personal power and enable you to contact your Higher Self and Guides and expand your spiritual awareness.

If you have never used guided meditations before you will find, in chapter one, all the information you need to work with this technique safely and easily. If you regularly use guided mediations, either alone or with a develop-ment group, then you will find this to be a useful source book.

There is no limit to the number of times you can use each inner journey. Each time you meditate you will find the experience richer and more fulfilling. The opportuni-ties for personal growth and self-transformation are limit-less. You have everything you need within you to heal yourself and to become the person you truly want to be. Use these guided journeys joyfully and trust yourself to know what you need.

CHAPTER 1 — UNDERSTANDING THE PROCESS

What is meditation? The dictionary definition is: '...an act of spiritual contemplation, to ponder, to muse.' Meditation is an integral part of many eastern religions. 'Traditional' meditation, as practised by Buddhists, Hindus and Christians alike is a very different process to 'guided' meditation.

Traditional meditation aims to quiet and calm the mind and often uses a mantra as a focus. *Om* and *Hare Krishna* are well known mantras, but any word or combination of words can be used. For example, *Love* or *Peace*, or *Be Still And Know*, or even something as mundane as *Milk Bottle Tops*, could all be used as mantras. The word or words used are irrelevant, as it is the process of repeating the word over and over again which is important. Traditional meditators may also choose to focus on the breath, a colour, a natural object such as a flower or a stone, an emotion or a specific thought such as, *I am the Source*. Some meditators may choose to 'observe with disinterest' the thoughts and emotions which arise during meditation, whilst others seek to erase all thoughts and enter a 'mental void'. This last type of meditation is extremely difficult as 'nothingness' may take years of practice to achieve.

I prefer to think of these types of meditations as unstructured, because there is no clearly defined beginning, middle and end. The main aim and purpose of this type of meditation is the stilling and calming of the mind and spirit.

Although traditional meditation has been proved to be extremely effective in reducing stress levels and promoting tranquillity and a sense of peace in the meditator, the main problem with the technique is that it requires concentrated and dedicated effort in order to produce worthwhile results. Anyone wishing to become a proficient meditator in this tradition must be prepared to spend a great deal of time, possibly years, before they can expect to reap the fruits of their efforts.

Guided meditations are altogether different. They are structured and have a precise beginning, middle and end. Each guided meditation is a self-contained experience, undertaken for a specific purpose. This might be self-healing, or absent healing for others, or to acquire specific answers to specific questions. Guided meditations require no practice and the benefits and results are immediate. This is because, rather than requiring the mind to be inactive and at rest, the mind is taken on an interesting and creative inner journey during which we can access forgotten or 'hidden' thoughts and feelings.

It is said (and I believe), that we have all the knowledge within us to solve our problems, make the right decisions and achieve peace, balance and harmony, both within our selves and with our relationship to the outer world around us. We already know everything we need to know because within each of us is a Wise One who knows who and what we are, and what we need to achieve our full potential.

There is a Hindu legend that tells of a time when the Gods wanted to preserve the most powerful, most sacred, most important Universal Knowledge. "Where can we put this knowledge to keep it safe?" they asked. Various suggestions were made. "The bottom of the deepest ocean," said one; and, "The top of the highest mountain," said another. "Scattered amongst the grains of sand within the driest desert," said a third; and, "Hidden between the roots of the oldest trees in the wildest forest," said a fourth; "Buried deep within the earth," said a fifth. None of these hiding places seemed appropriate as it was felt that the Universal Knowledge might too easily be found. At long last Brahma proposed the solution: "Let us put this knowledge inside the people... for they will never think to look inside themselves!"

This, of course, was the perfect solution, because it is true that people tend not to look within to find their own knowledge and power.

Guided meditations will lead you to your own wisdom, energy and creativity. They enable you to find your Wise One who will allow you to access the knowledge you already hold, to reveal and examine who you really are, what you really want and discover who you want to be and how to make the inner and outer changes necessary to achieve your goals. Guided meditations do this by helping you to 'switch off' the usually dominant left side of the brain, and 'switch on' the usually passive right side of the brain.

In the 1960s in California, USA, Roger Walcott Sperry and a group of his students, as a result of experiments aimed to assess the effects of surgery performed on epileptic patients, discovered that the right and left sides of the brain perform entirely different functions. Later studies conducted in other parts of the USA, France and Australia, confirmed Sperry's findings.

The left side of the brain is responsible for speech (patients who suffer a left-sided stroke find that they are speech-impaired), counting, reasoning, logic, analytical thinking, recognising time and space. The left side of the brain, which controls the right side of the body, is the dominant side of the brain.

The right side of the brain is responsible for recognising patterns, music, imagery, and art and emotions. The right side has no concept of time and space and is the intuitive, receptive, passive side, which controls the left side of the body.

We operate mostly from the left side of our brains for two reasons. The left side works faster than the right and our education system focuses on left brain skills: using words and numbers, thinking logically and analytically, being aware of time and space. Naturally, the more we use the left-hand side of the brain, the more practised and skilled it becomes, and the more it dominates the right side of the brain. As a result, the right side is not encouraged to operate. Additionally, tension and speed of thought and activity encourage the left brain to work even harder.

If you have ever been totally relaxed and totally involved in a creative process—writing, painting, making music, for example, where you are completely absorbed and the ideas just 'flow' without effort or conscious thought, then you have been functioning from the right side of the brain. By intentionally 'switching' to right brain functioning, we can access dormant power, creativity, knowledge, wisdom and skills.

This is the purpose of the guided meditations in this book.

Guided meditation 'ground rules'

It is important to observe a few common sense 'ground rules' when you embark on a guided meditation.

Ground rule— 1

Choose a time to meditate when you can make sure that you will be undisturbed. Take the phone off the hook or, if you prefer, switch on the answering machine. If you do decide to let the answering machine pick up you calls, always make sure that the phone bell is turned off. This is because you will be in a deeply relaxed state of mind, and the harsh jangling of the phone will disturb what will be a very enjoyable and informative experience. For the same reason, it is a good idea to close your doors to deter unwanted visitors, or to tell other people in the house what you are doing so that they do not disturb you.

Ground rule— 2

Dress comfortably. There are no 'right' or 'wrong' clothes for meditation, but it is best to wear whatever you feel most comfortable with: jeans, leggings, T-shirts, whatever, as long as they are loose, non-restrictive and comfortable.

Ground rule — 3

Don't attempt a guided meditation if you have been drinking alcohol or taking drugs. Although you can always return from your journey at any moment in time, and the worst that can happen is that you will fall asleep, it is always best to meditate when you are completely clear and in control.

Ground rule — 4

Allow sufficient time for the meditation. This means five minutes or so for 'settling in', plus the time it will take for the tape to play, plus another five to ten minutes to either record the experience in your meditation journal, or to just sit and think about what you have learned from the journey. Try to avoid the temptation of leaping up to make coffee/change the cat-litter/collect the children/send a fax or any of the other million and one things we fill our time with. This time is for you. You deserve it, so don't feel guilty.

Ground rule — 5

Choose a comfortable chair which will allow you to sit with your spine upright and both feet on the floor. It is best not to lie down to meditate as the chances are you will drift off to sleep. There is absolutely no need to sit on the floor with your legs folded in a half or full Lotus Position, unless this is completely comfortable for you, and your preferred way of being.

Ground rule — 6

Make sure you 'ground' properly at the end of the meditation. 'Grounding' is simply a technique for putting you back in touch with your physical being, the earth and the 'here and now' of the material world. Grounding is important because you will have been deeply involved with the sights, sounds and emotions of your inner world. Failure to make a conscious and definite re-connection with the outer world of objects and other people can result in a 'spacey' disconnected feeling. This can easily be avoided by grounding and techniques are given on page .

Ground rule — 7

Never, never, ever listen to a guided meditation tape whilst driving a car. You most certainly will not be able to make an inner journey whilst concentrating on driving, but nevertheless the tape could prove to be a dangerous distraction.

Ground rule — 8

Some people are able to visualise their inner journeys very clearly and can see the images in their 'mind's eye' as sharply and as brightly as if they were viewing a television screen. It is very important to recognise that not everyone has this facility and that people receive the images and impressions in different ways. For example, you may receive your impressions through physical sensations, emotional feelings or thoughts rather than pictures. Do not dismiss your impression just because you cannot 'see' the images. Your journey is valid for you, whatever form the experience takes.

Ground rule — 9

Please remember that you are in control of your guided journey and you can leave at any moment you choose. If you decide to finish the journey at any point, all you need to do is to open your eyes. Do remember, though, to ground, even if you have left the meditation and switched off the tape.

Keeping a meditation journal

I strongly recommend that you keep a journal of your guided meditations. Your journal will enable you to keep a record of your journeys and the thoughts and emotions connected with them. It is impossible to retain all the inner-work information in your head, and your journal will provide a record of ideas and insights. Over time, you will find it useful to be able to check back through your journal and observe the progress and changes you have made.

Any kind of notebook or loose-leaf ring-binder system can be used, but it is a good idea to choose paper and pens which you find satisfying and pleasurable to use. The notes you will make are about you, and for you, and are therefore very important.

I have found it best to use two pages of paper for each meditation. On the left-hand page I note down brief details of the journey, and on the right-hand page I make notes about my thoughts and feelings. There is always space left, and this is useful because it means I can return at a later date, if I choose, to note down additional information and ideas which may have occurred since completing the inner journey. Quite often, as a result of guided meditation, solutions to problems, new ways of looking at things and a deeper understanding of situations arise, and these are all worth recording.

Over the years I have kept records of most of my inner journeys. Looking back over the notes I have kept it is interesting to see which meditations proved to be most fruitful and rewarding, and the way in which my own understanding and development has expanded.

Choosing guided meditations

If you are new to guided meditations, I suggest you begin with meditations 1—4 taken from the self-healing section in chapter 2. Then, once you are familiar with the technique, you can choose to work with whichever of the meditations appeal to you most. All of the meditations can be repeated as many times as you choose and you may, in fact, find yourself working with just a few 'favourites'. On the other hand, you may decide to work through all of the meditations contained in the book. Either method is fine, and you should be guided by your intuition and do whatever feels right for you.

If you are an experienced meditator (either used to working alone or with a group), simply use this as a source-book, choosing the meditations which best suit your purpose.

Recording meditations

I have found it almost impossible to make an inner journey unless someone 'talks me through' the meditation. If you are working alone you will need to make a recording of the meditation before you begin. This will allow you to switch on the tape, listen and relax.

The most important thing to remember, when making a meditation tape, is to allow plenty of time for the inner journey images and conversations to appear and develop. So make sure you speak slowly and clearly, and leave long pauses between sentences. In each of the meditations I have indicated an appropriate length of time for these pauses. These are just approximations and can be lengthened or shortened to suit your own needs. For example, if I have indicated: ... (30 seconds), and you feel you would prefer to leave a longer or shorter gap of silence, then go right ahead.

Also, it is absolutely vital to label the tapes clearly and comprehensively. Speaking from experience, I can categorically say that it is extremely frustrating and irritating to find oneself under a waterfall when one had been looking forward to spending time in a crystal cave!

Entering and leaving guided meditations

There are a number of techniques you can use to get 'in' and 'out' of your inner journeys. I have listed a selection of introductions and departures/groundings in this section, rather than including them in the guided meditations themselves.

When you are making your tape-recording of a guided meditation:
- Select an introduction and record that (use the pause button to hold the tape);

- Select your guided meditation and record that (use the pause button to hold the tape);
- Select a departure/grounding and record that.

Your tape is now complete and ready to use.

You can use any of the introductions and departures with any of the guided meditations on a 'pick and mix' basis. Over time you will probably find there are certain descriptions which work best for you and these will become your usual way of getting 'in' and 'out'. If you are a newcomer to guided meditation I suggest you try a number of approaches to see which feel most comfortable.

Introduction

Each guided meditation requires an introduction which will relax and prepare you for your inner journey.

Introduction— 1

Sit quietly... (10 seconds) ...allow your body to settle into the chair... (20 seconds) ...feel where your body rests against the chair... (20 seconds) ...relax and allow the chair to carry your weight... (15 seconds) ...gently supporting you... (30 seconds) ...feel the soles of your feet supported on the ground, allow your eyes to close... (10 seconds) ...be aware of the rhythm of your breath... (30 seconds) ...follow your breath as you breathe in and breathe out... (30 seconds) ...focus on that gentle rhythm as your breath gently flows in and out... (30 seconds) ...and allow the cares and tensions of the day drop away from you... (30 seconds) ...you need do nothing except be in this safe space... (1 minute) ...now you are ready to begin...

Introduction— 2

Relax... (10 seconds) ...check that your body is aligned... (10 seconds) ...your spine is straight... (10 seconds) ... your feet firmly on the floor... (10 seconds) ...you are going to check your body for tension and

wherever you find it you will let it go... (20 seconds)
...you do not need tension in any part of your being...
(20 seconds) ...begin by taking a deep breath... (2 seconds) ...breathe in through your nose and out through
your mouth... (5 seconds) ...as you breath out, feel all the
tension of the day drain away... (10 seconds) ...take
another deep breath... (5 seconds) ...breathe out and
allow your eyes to close gently and naturally start by
checking your scalp and your hairline... (30 seconds)
...wherever you find tension just relax and let it go... (30
seconds) ...relax the muscles and release the tension...
(30 seconds) ...your forehead... (30 seconds) ...your eye-
lids and the tiny muscles at the corners of your eyes...
(30 seconds) ...relax and let go... (30 seconds) ...your jaw,
your tongue and your lips... (30 seconds) ...as you release
the tension allow your tongue to relax, your lips to part
slightly... (15 seconds) ...now check the back of your neck
and your shoulders... (30 seconds) ...if you find any
tightness or tension just let it go, you don't need it... (30
seconds) ...take another deep breath, a sigh... (5 seconds)
...now check your arms... (20 seconds) ...your hands and
fingers... (20 seconds) ...moving down to the chest, the
solar plexus, legs and feet ... (30 seconds) ...releasing
tension wherever you find it... (30 seconds) ...all should
be relaxed and comfortable... (15 seconds) ...now you are
ready to begin...

Introduction—3

Settle yourself comfortably... (10 seconds) ...your spine
should be straight, both feet firmly on the floor... (15
seconds) ...breathe in through your nose, out through
your mouth... (15 seconds) ...as you breathe in, you draw
in peace and calm... (8 seconds) ...as you breathe out,
you release the worries and cares you have been carrying... (8 seconds) ...as you breathe in, imagine you are
drawing light into the crown of your head... (10 seconds)
...a soothing, healing light which spreads down through
your body, into your heart centre... (15 seconds) ...and as
you breathe out you send all the negative energy you

have been holding, down, through your legs and into the soles of your feet, and down deep into the earth where it drains away... (20 seconds) ...gently breathing in healing, calming, peaceful light, clearing and cleansing... (30 seconds) ...breathing out all negative emotions, all stress and tension draining away, into the earth... (30 seconds) ...leaving you completely calm, completely clear, completely relaxed... (1 minute) ...now you are ready to begin...

Introduction—4

Sitting symmetrically, with your spine straight and both feet on the floor, begin by taking a deep breath... (8 seconds) ...breathe in peace and tranquillity... (8 seconds) ...breathe out and release tension... (8 seconds) ...tense the muscles in your forehead... (10 seconds) ...around your eyes... (10 seconds) ...your jaw muscles... (10 seconds) ...clench your teeth... (10 seconds) ...feel the tightness... (5 seconds) ...now release, relax and let go... (20 seconds) ...feel the tightness and the tension drain away ... (20 seconds) ...continue to breathe gently and naturally... (30 seconds) ...breathing in peace and tranquillity, breathing out any tension or stress you may be holding... (1 minute) ...shrug your shoulders, tense the muscles and lift your shoulders up towards your ears... (15 seconds) ...feel the tension and the muscle-strain, hold that position... (10 seconds) ...now relax... (20 seconds) ...let your shoulders drop down to a comfortably position and feel the tension drain away... (30 seconds) ...tense the muscles in your arms and hands... (10 seconds) ...make a fist with each hand... (10 seconds) ...tighten and hold the muscles... (10 seconds) ...now relax and release... (30 seconds) ...tighten your abdomen... (5 seconds) ...thigh and buttock muscles... (5 seconds) ...your legs and feet... (15 seconds) ...release and let go... (30 seconds) ...settle into your space more comfortably... (1 minute... feeling calm and relaxed... (1 minute) ...now you are ready to begin...

If you are unfamiliar with the chakras I suggest you read Chapter 3, Chakra guided meditation, *before using introductions nos.5 and 6.*

Centre yourself in your space and align your body... (1 minute) ...making sure your spine is straight and both feet are firmly on the floor... (30 seconds) ...breathe in... (10 seconds) ...and breathe out... (10 seconds) ...breathe gently and follow the flow of your breath... (1 minute) ...become aware of your crown chakra... (30 seconds) ...allow it to open gently... (1 minute) ...move down to your brow chakra... (30 seconds) ...is it spinning right to left... (10 seconds) ...left to right?... (10 seconds) ...allow it to open gently... (1 minute) ...move to your throat chakra... (30 seconds) ...balance and align your throat chakra with your brow chakra... (1 minute) ...focus now on your heart chakra... (30 seconds) ...allow it to open gently... (1 minute) ...balance and align... (1 minute) ...move to the solar plexus... (10 seconds) ...continue to breathe gently and rhythmically... (30 seconds) ...allow your solar plexus to open gently... (1 minute) ...balance and align... (1 minute) ...become aware of your sacral chakra... (10 seconds) ...allow your sacral to open gently... (1 minute) ...balance and align... (1 minute) ...finally move down to your root chakra... (10 seconds) ...allow your root to open gently... (1 minute) ...balance and align... (1 minute) ...breathe gently and easily... (30 seconds) ...imagine a stream of golden light entering your crown chakra... (10 seconds) ...moving down through the brow... (10 seconds) ...the throat... (10 seconds) ...the heart... (10 seconds) ...the solar plexus... (10 seconds) ...the sacral... (10 seconds) ...the root... (10 seconds) ...streaming into the earth, cleansing and clearing... (15 seconds) ...be aware of the gentle flow of your breath... (30 seconds) ...now you are ready to begin...

Sit comfortably, making sure that your spine is straight, your body is symmetrical and both feet are firmly on the floor... (30 seconds) ...breathe in deeply and exhale... (20 seconds) ...continue to breath gently, releasing tension on every out breath... (20 seconds) ...focus on your breathing, becoming aware of the gentle flow of your breath... (30 seconds) ...imagine a cord of clear silver-white energy running from your root chakra at the base of your spine... (20 seconds) ...see the cord split into two cords which run down your legs and into the soles of your feet... (30 seconds) ...and down, down deep into the centre of the earth... (30 seconds) ...these are your grounding cords which will hold you firmly connected to the earth whilst you take this inner journey... (10 seconds) ...continue to breath gently... (30 seconds) ...relax, open and balance the heart and throat chakras... (1 minute) ...the solar plexus and the brow chakras... (1 minute) ...the root and the crown chakras... (1 minute) ...breathe deeply... (30 seconds) ...now you are ready to begin...

Departure/grounding

Always record a departure/grounding at the end of each guided meditation. Grounding is extremely important as the process will 'earth' you back in the outer reality of the day-to-day world.

Departure/grounding — 1

Now you are ready to return to your outer reality... (30 seconds) ...open your eyes and look around the room... (15 seconds) ...be aware of the chair you are sitting on... (10 seconds) ...the floor upon which your feet are resting... (10 seconds) ...flex your fingers and toes... (10 seconds) ...stretch... (20 seconds) ...stamp the ground, first with the right foot... (5 seconds) ...and then with the left foot... (5 seconds)

Departure/grounding—2

Now you are ready to leave this inner space... (30 seconds) ...become aware of the rhythm of your breath... (1 minute) ...as with each breath you become more focused and more centred in the reality of the everyday world... (30 seconds) ...open your eyes and focus on your feet... (5 seconds) ...where they touch the floor... (5 seconds) ...make a conscious connection between the soles of your feet and the ground beneath your feet... (20 seconds) ...be aware of the connection between your self and the earth... (30 seconds) ...and now you are ready to return to your daily life...

Departure/grounding—3

Now you are ready to return to the everyday world... (30 seconds) ...focus your attention on your breath and become aware of your body... (1 minute) ...particularly feel where your body rests on the chair and where your feet rest on the ground... (30 seconds) ...imagine your feet are growing roots which reach right down through the earth and into the centre of the earth... (30 seconds) ...concentrate on the connection between your self and the earth beneath your feet... (30 seconds) .....open your eyes and become aware of the sights and sounds of the room... (20 seconds) ...and the world outside the room... (20 seconds)

Departure/grounding—4

Now you are ready to return to your everyday surroundings... (30 seconds) ...become aware of your body... (10 seconds) ...and your breath... (10 seconds) ...and your feet where they are firmly in contact with the ground... (10 seconds) ...imagine a silver-white cord which stretches from the base of your spine, down through your legs and feet, deep, deep into the earth... (30 seconds) ...this grounding cord holds you firmly to the earth and is your connection the earth's energy... (20 seconds) ...open your eyes and look around you...

Departure/grounding—5

If you are unfamiliar with the chakras, I suggest you read chapter four, Chakra guided meditations *before using Departures/groundings nos.5 and 6.*

Now you are ready to leave this inner space and return to your outer reality... (30 seconds) ...return your attention to your body... (30 seconds) ...become aware of your chakras... (5 seconds) ...beginning with the root chakra, allow each chakra to close as much or as little as you choose... (5 seconds) ...move upwards from the root... (10 seconds) ...to the sacral... (10 seconds) ...to the solar plexus... (10 seconds) ...to the heart... (10 seconds) ...to the brow... (10 seconds) ...and, finally to the crown... (20 seconds) ...when you are satisfied that each chakra is closed and balanced to your satisfaction picture a spiral of golden light encircling your body from the top of your head to the soles of your feet... (30 seconds) ...you are encased in a bubble of golden light... (20 seconds) ...now become aware of your connection to the earth... (10 seconds) ...feel that connection through the soles of your feet... (15 seconds) ...open your eyes and return to your day-to-day surroundings.

Departure/grounding—6

Now you are ready to leave this inner journey... (30 seconds) ...focus on your breath and with every breath you take you become more centred in your everyday surroundings... (1 minute) ...check your chakras... (5 seconds) ...are they balanced?... (30 seconds) ...are they aligned?... (30 seconds) ...are they as open or as closed as you want them to be?... (30 seconds) ...work on each chakra in turn, and place a cross of light in a circle of light over each, the crown... (10 seconds) ...the brow... (10 seconds) ...the throat... (10 seconds) ...the heart... (10 seconds) ...the solar plexus... (10 seconds) ...the sacral... (10 seconds) ...the root... (10 seconds) ...send your grounding cord down, from your sacral chakra deep into the core of the earth... (20 seconds) ...to hold and anchor you firmly in this incarnation and to retain your connection with the earth's energy... (10 seconds) ...and finally step into a suit of light...(15 seconds) ...draw on gloves of light... (10 seconds) ...and shoes of light... (10 seconds) ...and wrap a turban of light about your head... (10 seconds) ...open your eyes and centre yourself in your daily reality.

Guided Meditation Checklist

Before you begin your guided meditation make sure that:
1. You have your tape—which includes an introduction, the meditation, the departure/grounding.
2. The phone is switched off and you won't be disturbed.
3. You have allowed sufficient time to complete the guided meditation.
4. You haven't been drinking alcohol or taking unprescribed drugs.
5. You are comfortable and warm.

CHAPTER 2 —
SELF-HEALING

I love you, whether you know it or not
I love you, whether I show it or not
There are so many things I'd like to say inside my heart
And now is a good time to start

Universal Chant

Before we can even think about healing other people, our relationships or the planet, we need to invest time and energy in our own self-healing. For it is only when we are functioning from a balanced and healthy inner space that we can give healing to others.

Unfortunately, we are taught from an early age that loving and nurturing ourselves is somehow 'wrong' and that our care and attention should be directed outwards, to the world around us, not inwards to ourselves. As a result of this conditioning we tend to ignore our own needs, and feel 'guilty' if we give time to ourselves. This thinking manifests itself as the *I Just Don't Have Time For Me* syndrome or the *Everyone Is More Important Than Me* model; two common conditions which afflict us all from to time.

We rush from one task to another, hurrying to meet deadlines, extending the day from early morning to late at night so that we can 'get everything done' and meet everyone's needs and expectations. We make sure we fill every moment with activity and sound because, of course, in stillness and silence we have the opportunity to meet ourselves. And, sadly, quite often we are not on good terms with ourselves. Finally, when we no longer have the energy—either mental, physical or emotional—to meet the demands which are placed on us, (both by others and by ourselves), exhaustion takes over. Then we feel empty and irritable. Our responsibilities weigh us down, our joy in life and living drains away, and still we feel guilty because we tell ourselves we should and we ought to be able to cope. Does any of this sound familiar?

In order to initiate the self-healing process, begin by accepting that the most important relationship in your life, indeed, the most important relationship you will ever have, is your relationship with yourself. You need to invest the same amount of time and energy in building and nurturing the relationship with yourself that you would invest in any other significant relationship in your life. In the same way that you work at making relationships right with other people, you need to work at making the relationship with yourself the very best you can.

The first step to self-healing and to improving your relationship with yourself is to recognise and accept that, on a regular basis, you need to take personal time-out. Time for yourself. Time to rest and relax, refresh your body, mind and spirit and regain your inner balance. Only then, when you are balanced in your inner space and grounded in the outer world around you, can you face daily living with tranquillity, courage and confidence.

The guided meditations which follow are designed to help you achieve that inner balance. You may find that you are immediately drawn to some of the meditations and that you want to use them on a regular, day-to-day basis. Many people devise their own daily self-healing programme. Other meditations may seem more appropriate for occasional use, or for group-work.

You will know best what you need. Allow your intuition to guide you. Your own inner Wise One will always produce the appropriate guidance providing, of course, you take the time to ask and to listen to the answer.

1. Energised guided meditation

• To release tension and gain energy and vitality.

Switch on your tape-recorder; open with chosen introduction.

Imagine you are walking in a meadow... (30 seconds) The sun is shining and the sky above is a wonderful clear blue... (30 seconds) Here and there you can see a cloud, a small white puffball floating across the blue sky... (30 seconds) And you feel a warm breeze on your skin... (15 seconds) As you walk you feel the clean, fresh grass under your feet... (30 seconds) Take a moment or two to look around... (30 seconds) Listen to the birds, feel the sun, smell the fragrance of the flowers... (1 minute) All is peaceful, all is safe in this very special place... (30 seconds) A little way ahead, there are trees and you walk towards them... (30 seconds) Knowing you are alone, but completely safe... (15 seconds) You enter the wooded glade... (15 seconds) You walk between the trees... (30 seconds) And the sunlight shines down through the leaves and branches, making a a pattern all around... (20 seconds) There are flowers everywhere... (30 seconds) Rich colours... (15 seconds) And the fragrance of flowers is on the air... (30 seconds) There is a stream close by... (15 seconds) You can hear the water making a gentle rushing sound... (20 seconds) You walk to the riverbank where the stream flows gently... (30 seconds) The water is crystal clear and the sunlight reflects a sparkling pattern... (30 seconds) You walk down the gently sloping bank into the stream... (20 seconds) The water is warm and very shallow... (10 seconds) It laps gently around your ankles... (20 seconds) You wade through the water, walking on clean, soft sand which is level, and firm underfoot... (30 seconds) As you walk the sun warms you... (30 seconds) Ahead is a waterfall, fresh, clear water cascading down in sparkling layers... (10 seconds) You walk towards it... (30 seconds) Stand beneath it... (30 seconds) The waterfall is warm... (10 seconds) You feel the clear, sparkling water cascading down around you... (30 seconds) Clearing and cleansing... (30

seconds) Energising... (30 seconds) Strength and energy and vitality pour into every part of your being... (1 minute) Your body, mind and spirit are refreshed and renwed... (30 seconds) Opening your eyes you see a double rainbow, arcing down from the sky; and the colours of the rainbow, red, orange, yellow, green, blue, indigo, violet, join with the waterfall... (1 minute) Every fibre of your being is cleansed and cleared and renewed... (1 minute) . You are filled with energy... (1 minute) Strengthened and revitalised... (1 minute) When you are ready, leave the waterfall... (30 seconds) Begin to re-trace your steps... (30 seconds) Back through the stream... (30 seconds) Up the gently sloping bank... (30 seconds) Past the flowers, through the trees... (30 seconds) Knowing that you can return to the energising waterfall at any time you choose... (30 seconds) Out into the meadow again, to the place where you began this healing inner journey... (30 seconds)
Close with chosen departure/grounding.

2. Inner peace guided meditation
• To restore inner peace and tranquillity.

Switch on your tape-recorder; open with chosen introduction.
Imagine you are walking along a beach... (30 seconds) It is early evening and the white sand is still warm from the day's sun... (30 seconds) Above, the sky is fading to deep blue... (15 seconds) The horizon is streaked with rose and crimson, cast by the setting sun... (30 seconds) Waves roll in from the sea and spread onto the white sand... (30 seconds) Sparkling and foaming about your feet... (20 seconds) You hear the sound of the ocean... (30 seconds) And the cry of the gulls over the water... (20 seconds) And you are completely at peace... (30 seconds) To your right is the entrance to a cave and you walk forward, across the sand, to investigate... (1 minute) There is a soft, welcoming glow illuminating

the mouth of the cave, and so you enter... (20 seconds) You walk forward, into the cave... (20 seconds) And see that the walls and floor are crystal... (30 seconds) You are inside an amethyst crystal cave... (30 seconds) You are walking on a pale-lilac marble pathway which is smooth and slightly warm underfoot... (15 seconds) All about you the flames of a hundred candles light the walls which sparkle with crystalline light... (30 seconds) Reflecting the dancing candle flames all about you... (20 seconds) In the centre of the cave is a seat... (10 seconds) You sit down, knowing that this cave is completely safe... (20 seconds) Aware that here in this very special crystal cave you are completely protected... (30 seconds) Take a moment to enjoy the peace and serenity... (1 minute) Walking towards you is a Guardian, cloaked in white Light... (30 seconds) Someone who has taken care of you for a very long time... (20 seconds) Someone who cares for you in a very special way and who is dedicated to your protection... (20 seconds) Your Guardian smiles, gently, and you feel cloaked in love and Light... (30 seconds) Completely accepted and acknowledged... (30 seconds) Your Guardian's hand is laid. gently and lovingly on your brow... (30 seconds) And you feel a great sense of peace and tranquillity... (30 seconds) A stream of Light and love enters your consciousness... (30 seconds) Soothing away the turmoil, the anxiety, the fear... (30 seconds) There is peace now, an inner tranquillity which has replaced all the confusion and distress... (15 seconds) Feel the calm, the love and the Light streaming through every part of your being... (20 seconds) Clearing, cleansing, releasing and healing... (30 seconds) Be aware now of a sense of perfect peace... (30 seconds) And accept this gentle healing... (3 minutes) Now your Guardian has completed the healing... (15 seconds) And it is time for you to leave the crystal cave... (20 seconds) Take a moment to thank your Guardian... (30 seconds) And retrace your steps back along the marble pathway to the cave entrance... (30 seconds) Knowing that, now you have found the crystal cave, you may return here whenever you choose... (10 seconds) Whenever you wish to restore your inner peace and tranquillity... (10 seconds) Move out through the cave entrance, back onto the beach... (20 seconds) Where the velvet blue sky is now shimmering with stars... (10 seconds) And the moon shines her gentle radiance to light your way... (10 seconds) Walk back along the moonlit beach... (20 seconds) Until you reach the place where this healing inner journey began... (30 seconds)

Close with chosen departure/grounding.

3 [A] Forgiveness and cleansing guided meditation

• To forgive yourself and to cleanse away guilt and other negative emotions.

Switch on your tape-recorder; open with chosen introduction.

You find yourself walking in the desert... (30 seconds) All about you are soft, undulating sand dunes... (20 seconds) It is late afternoon and the sun is low in the sky... (20 seconds) A gentle breeze blows to cool you, softening the heat of the day... (15 seconds) A little way ahead you see palm trees and you walk towards them... (30 seconds) Knowing that the oasis is your destination... (15 seconds) As you approach you see that, although the oasis is deserted, someone has prepared a place for you... (30 seconds) Beside the pool of shimmering water you find silken cushions, a silver goblet and a jug of clear, golden liquid... (30 seconds) Sink down onto the cushions and look around you... (1 minute) Notice the palm trees silhouetted against the orange sky... (30 seconds) The flowers growing about the waterside... (30 seconds) A desert hawk flies overhead, spreading its wings in greeting... (30 seconds) The water looks cool and inviting and you lean forward and look into the clear depths of the pool... (1 minute) The pool is clear and clean... (15 seconds) The sparkling water invites you in... (10 seconds) You ease yourself into

the water and float gently... (2 minutes) Allow the water to hold you... (1 minute) And wash over you... (1 minute) Floating, you feel all the guilt, all the fear, all the negative emotions being washed away... (2 minutes) You know that you are being cleansed and cleared at all levels of your being... (30 seconds) Remain in the water for as long as you choose, just floating gently, effortlessly... (3 or 4 minutes) When you are ready, leave the pool of self-forgiveness... (30 seconds) Sit at the waterside and allow the soft rays of the sun to dry you... (30 seconds) Now pour the golden water of purification into the silver goblet... (10 seconds) Sip the liquid... (10 seconds) And as you drink you are filled with a sense of peace and serenity... (30 seconds) You have washed away the past and you can walk into the future with courage and certainty... (30 seconds) Renewed and restored... (30 seconds) Take one more look around you, knowing that you may return to bathe in the pool of self-forgiveness and drink the water of purification at any time you choose... (25 seconds) When you are ready, retrace your steps... (20 seconds) Away from the oasis... (20 seconds) Back through the sand dunes... (30 seconds) To the place where this healing inner journey began..
Close with chosen departure/grounding.

3 [B] Forgiveness and cleansing guided meditation

- To forgive yourself and cleanse guilt and other negative emotions.

Switch on your tape-recorder; open with chosen introduction.

You find yourself on a hillside... (20 seconds) Walking towards a small cave entrance which is set into the rocky escarpment which rises up ahead of you... (30 seconds) The sun is low in the sky and a slight breeze cools you as you climb higher... (30 seconds) Now you are at the cave entrance... (10 seconds) You step inside... (15 seconds) The cavern is cool and lit with torches which are set into sconces in the wall... (30 seconds) In the centre of the cavern there is a circle of stones and within the circle a shaft of violet and gold light streams down... (30 seconds) The violet and gold mix and intermingle and you know that this is the light of forgiveness and cleansing... (30 seconds) You move forward and step over the stones, into the centre of the circle The light streams down, around you and through you... (1 minute) And you feel it cool and clear and cleansing... (1 minute) You watch as the gold blends with the violet... (1 minute) Cleansing and clearing away all the guilt, all the envy, all the negative emotions... (2 minutes) All are washed away by the light of forgiveness... (1 minute) You stretch upwards to the gold and violet light which cascades around your head and streams down and through your body... (30 seconds) Cleansing and clearing at all levels of your being... (30 seconds) You watch as the violet and gold light changes to silver and you know that this is the light of purification... (30 seconds) Stand and allow the silver light to permeate every cell of your being... (3—4 minutes) Bringing you calmness and peace and complete tranquillity... (2 minutes) Be aware that you are now cleansed of the past and you can leave this cavern purified and renewed... (1 minutes) Take a few more moments to experience the healing power of the silver light and the tranquillity and protection of the cavern... (3—4 minutes) Then, when you are ready, step out of the circle... (1 minute) Knowing that you can return to the violet and gold and silver light whenever you choose... (30 seconds) Now re-trace your steps, back to the cave entrance... (30 seconds) Out onto the hillside, under the velvet blue sky... (30 seconds) Make your way down the hill, by the gentle light of the moon... (30 seconds) . Back to where this healing inner journey began... (15 seconds)

Close with chosen departure/grounding.

4. Healing your Inner Child guided meditation

- To re-connect with and to make amends to your Inner Child for hurtful and distressing childhood experiences.

Switch on your tape-recorder; open with chosen introduction. Imagine that you are sitting on a beach... (30 seconds) Watching the tide ebb and flow across the white sand... (30 seconds) Listen to the sound of the waves breaking on the shore, and the call of the gulls flying high overhead... (30 seconds) Smell the ocean... (30 seconds) Take a few moments to relax and enjoy the peace and the calm... (1—2 minutes) Looking down the beach you see a small child walking beside the shoreline... (30 seconds) The child is walking towards you... (1 minute) Wait patiently for the child to approach... (1 minute) As the child moves nearer towards you, you see that this small person is really you, when you were just five years old... (1 minute) Your heart swells with love for this small child and you stand, brush off the sand, and walk towards your child... (1 minute) Your child waves to you and begins to run towards you... (30 seconds) Now you are both smiling... (30 seconds) You meet... (30 seconds) You kneel down on the sand and gently, tenderly, carefully, place your arms around your child... (1 minute) You hug your child, and your child hugs you back... (30 seconds) There is a wonderful outpouring of love between the two of you... (2—3 minutes) Holding your child gently, you look into your child's eyes and say, "I love you..."... (2 minutes) Now you have the opportunity to tell your child everything you have always wanted to say... (10 seconds) Maybe you want to apologise for events in your childhood... (10 seconds) Or perhaps you want to reassure your child that he/she is really loved... (10 seconds) Or maybe you want to say that you will always be there for your child, and you will never leave or hurt your child ever again... (10 seconds) Take as much time as you need to say all the things you want to say... (10 seconds) And to hold and comfort your child... (10 seconds) To give your child the warmth and under- standing, the acceptance and love which your child has missed out on... (5 minutes) You may like to create a dialogue with your child by asking questions... (5 sec- onds) Whatever you ask, listen very carefully when your child answers, and treat your child with care and tender- ness and respect... (5 minutes) When you are ready become aware of an energy which is forming in your heart centre... (2 minutes) This energy is the essence of the love you have for your child... (10 seconds) Gradually the energy, which you can see is pink and sparkling, expands to form a bubble of pink light which encompasses you and your child... (1 minute) You hold your child as the pink light soothes and warms both of you... (1 minute) And you are both reunited in love and tenderness for one another... (2 minutes) Now it is time to say good-bye to your child, but you know that you can return to love and be with your child at any time you choose... (30 seconds) Say good-bye... (1 minute) And watch as your child walks back along the shoreline, turn- ing to wave to you, smiling and happy... (30 seconds) Turn and make your way back along the beach... (30 sec- onds) To the place where this healing inner journey began... (30 seconds)

Close with chosen departure/grounding.

5. Dealing with physical pain guided meditation

- To combat physical pain and speed the self-healing process. **Important note:** This guided meditation is not intended to replace medical treatment. Instead, this meditation should be used **in conjunc- tion with** your regular treatment, whether conven- tional/allopathic, homeopathic or herbal.

Switch on your tape-recorder; open with chosen introduction.

Imagine that you are walking in the countryside... (30 seconds) All about you is the healing green of trees and plants... (30 seconds) Fragrant flowers fill the air with their perfume... (30 seconds) The sun shines in a clear blue sky... (30 seconds) And you are filled with a sense of peace and serenity... (1 minute) Ahead you see a small pyramid-shaped building... (15 seconds) Walk towards it... (30 seconds) As you approach, a section of the pyramid slides open to create a doorway... (30 seconds) You step inside and the first thing you notice is the perfume... (30 seconds) And the gentle golden light... (30 seconds) In the centre of the pyramid chamber there is a large, soft cushion and, placed on the cushion, there is a robe... (30 seconds) This is a transparent gossamer robe of gold and silver thread... (30 seconds) Walk towards it, pick it up... (30 seconds) Slip on the robe and immediately sense the healing energy which is woven into every strand and every fibre... (1 minute) You sit on the cushion and allow yourself to relax... (30 seconds) Breathing the fragrant perfume and being washed by the gentle golden light... (30 seconds) Close your eyes for a moment... (1 minute) Now open them and see a globe of shimmering golden light hovering in the air, directly in front of you at eye-level... (30 seconds) You can direct this golden light to any part of your physical being for additional healing... (30 seconds) Where do you need healing?... (30 seconds) Direct the golden light... (10 seconds) You will see that you can increase or decrease the size of the globe just by thinking it larger or smaller... (30 seconds) You may want to expand the globe of golden light so that you are sitting at the centre of the healing light... (1 minute) Or you may want to direct it to just one part of your body... (1 minute) Wherever the golden globe of healing light touches you, you feel cool healing energy... (1 minute) Take as much time as you need... (5 seconds) This golden light is boundless and unlimited... (5 seconds) Allow the golden light to work on your body... (5 seconds) Dissolving pain and healing wherever it touches... (5—10 minutes)

When you are ready gather the healing energy back into a globe and send it up to the apex of the pyramid, high above your head... (30 seconds) Remove the gold and silver robe and lay it on the cushion... (30 seconds) Take one last look around the pyramid chamber, sensing the peace and tranquillity and healing energy... (30 seconds) Knowing that, now you have found this pyramid you may return for healing at any time you choose... (30 seconds) Now leave the pyramid... (30 seconds) Making sure that the entrance closes behind you... (15 seconds) And, back out into the sunlight, make your way back to the place where this healing inner journey began... (30 seconds) Close with chosen departure/grounding.

6. RELEASING ANGER GUIDED MEDITATION
• To let go of anger.

Switch on your tape-recorder; open with chosen introduction.

Imagine that you are sitting beside a fountain... (30 seconds) Watching the sparkling water cascading down into a blue marble basin... (30 seconds) Just watch the water bubble and rush and flow... (30 seconds) And listen to the gentle sound it makes... (30 seconds) Notice the way the water forms bubbles... (30 seconds) As you watch, see the bubbles become larger on the surface of the water... (30 seconds) Now the surface of the water is covered with pale blue bubbles... (30 seconds) Bubbles of every size, from very small to very large... (1 minute) Begin to pay particular attention to just one bubble which has caught your eye... (30 seconds) Watch as your special bubble floats and bobs on the water... (30 seconds) Reaching out you take the bubble on the palm of your hand... (30 seconds) The bubble rests there... (30 seconds) Become aware that your special blue bubble is beginning to expand... (30 seconds) Becoming larger and larger... (1 minute) Until it is large enough for you to step inside... (1 minute) You find yourself inside the blue bubble... (30 seconds) In the centre of the bubble is a box... (30 seconds) Open the lid and you will find that is completely empty... (30 seconds) Place your hands inside the box and focus all of your energy on your anger... (1 minute) The anger you have been carrying within you for such a long time... (30 seconds) Now concentrate on gathering your anger and sending it down, into your hands, into your fingertips... (2 minutes) Watch as your anger streams into the empty box... (2 minutes) Be patient and watch as the box begins to fill with your anger... (2 minutes) What colour is your anger?... (30 seconds) What consistency is it?... (30 seconds) Is it hot or cold?... (30 seconds) Notice that as your anger continues to stream from your fingertips, the box expands... (2 minute) So that the box becomes large enough to contain all of it... (30 seconds) When you are sure that all your anger has cleared and drained into the box, close the lid... (1 minute) Notice that once the lid is closed it forms a tight seal so that none of your anger can escape... (15 seconds) Put the box down... (10 seconds) Now look around you and notice there is a small doorway, just large enough for you to walk through... (15 seconds) Go through the doorway and find yourself once more beside the fountain... (30 seconds) You are standing beside the blue bubble which holds the box containing your anger, and this blue bubble has now shrunk back to its original, small, bubble-size... (30 seconds) With your right hand pick up the bubble and place it on the palm of your left hand... (20 seconds) Gently breathe on the bubble and watch it begin to shrink... (30 seconds) Watch as the bubble becomes smaller and smaller and smaller until, finally, it melts and disappears... (1 minute) Remain beside the fountain for a few moments more... (30 seconds) Listening to the gentle sound of the water as it cascades into the blue marble basin... (1 minute) Becoming aware that an inner peace and tranquillity have replaced your anger... (2 minutes) Now you are ready to leave this healing inner journey, knowing that you can return to the fountain at any time you choose... (30 seconds) Close with chosen departure/grounding.

7. Releasing unborn children

• For releasing guilt and fear connected with pregnancy termination.

Switch on your tape-recorder; open with chosen introduction.
You are sitting in a garden... (30 seconds) Surrounded by flowers... (30 seconds) Roses... (10 seconds) ...tulips... (10 seconds) ...lilies...orchids... (10 seconds) ...marigolds... (5 seconds) ...daisies... (5 seconds) ...every flower of every colour and type imaginable... (10 seconds) The fragrance of each flower blends into a wonderful, heady fragrance... (30 seconds) The colours range from the purest white to the deepest red... (30 seconds) ...clear blue, pale lemon, dazzling pink, subtle apricot... (30 seconds) And there is healing green all around you... (1 minute) ...the green of the grass and the leaves on the flowers and the bushes and the trees... (1 minute) Tiny birds perch on the branches of the trees, filling the air with their song... (1 minute).. Sit for a while and simply breathe the perfume, absorb the colours and enjoy the beauty which is all around you... (2 minutes) Be at peace in this calm, still, beautiful garden... (30 seconds) Relaxing even more, you see your Guide walking towards you... (30 seconds).. As this dazzling Being of Light approaches, sending you love and acceptance, you feel blessed by this presence... (1 minute) Knowing that your Guide understands, accepts and loves you unconditionally... (30 seconds) There is nothing which you have done, nothing you have thought, nothing you have experienced, nothing you have desired which your Guide does not know about... (1 minute) Yet this Being of Light accepts you completely and loves you unconditionally... (30 seconds) Your Guide sits next to you and you gaze into your Guide's eyes... (1 minute).. Seeing there only absolute unconditional love... (1 minute) Gently your Guide takes hold of your hand... (10 seconds) At the contact you feel a surge of healing energy... (30 seconds) Your Guide now hands you a heart-shaped rose-quartz crystal... (30 sec-

onds) . As you hold the crystal you feel it surge and vibrate with energy... (2 minutes).. Gently, tenderly, your Guide explains that this crystal holds the energy of your unborn child or children... (2 minutes) And that you now have the opportunity to say, directly, everything you would have said before, if you could have had the opportunity... (30 seconds) You now have the chance to make your peace with your unborn child or children... (30 seconds) Do you want to speak of love?... (10 seconds) Do you want to ask for forgiveness?... (10 seconds) Do you want to explain to your unborn child or children why you were unable to allow them to incarnate?... (10 seconds) Do you want to say what you have learned from the experience?... (10 seconds) Take your time to say whatever you need to say... (30 seconds) Pour out your heart... (6—7 minutes) When you have said everything there is to say you will see that the rose-quartz crystal you are holding will begin to grow warm in your hands... (30 seconds) Watch carefully and you will see the crystal begin to gently vibrate... (1 minute) As it vibrates it begins to hum gently... (30 seconds) A low, gentle, healing sound... (30 seconds) Watch as a pink light forms around the crystal... (30 seconds) ...like a pale, rosy aura... (30 seconds) As you watch, see this pink light of forgiveness form into a stream of light which enters your heart chakra, soothing and healing... (3 minutes) Experience complete understanding of the situation... (3 minutes) You are bathed in absolute forgiveness and pure unconditional love... (3 minutes) Feel the warmth of the rose pink light... (30 seconds) Be aware of the gentle healing sound... (30 seconds) Know that your unborn child or children are filled with unconditional love, understanding and acceptance for you... (2 minutes) All is well... (2 minutes) When you are ready, you return the heart-shaped rose-quartz crystal to your Guide... (30 seconds) Your Guide may have a message for you... (5 seconds) If so, listen carefully... (3 minutes).. When you are ready, thank your Guide and say goodbye... (1 minute).. Watch as your Guide leaves you... (30

seconds) Sit a little while longer in the garden, enjoying the colours and the perfume and the birdsong... (2 minutes) And then, when you are ready, prepare to leave this healing inner journey... (30 seconds)
Close with chosen departure/grounding.

CHAPTER 3— HEALING

I am a circle
I am healing you
You are a circle
You are healing me
Unite us
Be one
Unite us
Be as one

Native American Chant

In the previous chapter you looked at the ways in which you can use guided meditation for self-healing. Because we all interconnect at a vibratory and energy level, it is also possible to heal others, and our relationships with them, through guided meditation.

Guided meditations achieve the desired result because, when creative energy is directed towards a specific person, with a specific intent, that energy can be received and transmuted. Think about the transmission of radio waves. They are in the air all about us, all the time, twenty-four hours each day. If we do not have the radio switched on, then we are completely unaware of them. Once we press the switch, though, the waves are transmuted into music or conversation. In the same way, the energy you send out can be picked up by another person, on a higher vibratory level, and transmuted through the chakras to manifest in the physical world.

One word of caution, though. The energy you use is powerful. Do not, under any circumstances, for any reason, attempt to use that energy for anything other than good. Aside from any other reason (and there are many), you should be aware that negative energy will always rebound on the sender, one way or another. So, if you attempt to 'ill-wish' another through guided meditation, be assured that whatever you send them will return to you, with bells on!

The following meditations are completely safe, both for the sender and the receiver, and can bring about positive changes in all kinds of relationships and situations.

1. RELEASING AND HEALING RELATIONSHIPS FROM THE PAST GUIDED MEDITATION

- To release and heal others from the past who may have become involved in negative relationships with you (for example, partners, lovers, friends, children, parents, employers, colleagues).
- Note: like all the meditations, this inner journey may be repeated as many time as you like. So, you may prefer to deal with one relationship at a time or, you may prefer to work with a number of relationships at once. Before you begin the meditation, consider what feels right for you, and then follow your intuition.

Switch on your tape-recorder; open with chosen introduction.
Imagine you are standing in a clear space... (15 seconds) Draw a white circle on the ground around you... (15 seconds) You can use any substance to draw the circle, paint or light or something else of your own choosing... (20 seconds) Make sure the circle is completely closed and that you are standing in the centre... (1 minute) Now draw another circle, directly in front of your first circle... (25 seconds) Making sure that the circle in front of you does not touch or overlap the circle in which you are standing... (25 seconds) Now place inside the circle in front of you the person or people you wish to make your peace with, release and heal... (1 minute) As you place each person inside the circle, you may notice that there are cords, chains or ties connecting you to them... (30 seconds) If this is the case, don't worry, this is perfectly normal, in fact, if the relationship has

been very negative, you can expect to see a number of attachments between yourself and the other person... (10 seconds) Explain to each person in turn that you wish to make your peace with them and release them from this negative relationship, and that you want to heal the relationship between the two of you. Take as long as you need to say this... (3—4 minutes for each person) Now speak to each person in the circle and tell them that you forgive them for any hurt or harm they may have caused you... (3—4 minutes for each person) And ask for forgiveness from them for any hurt or harm you may have caused them... (3—4 minutes for each person) Now it is time to remove the attachments which hold you to each person in the circle. Imagine you have a pair of extremely sharp scissors... (10 seconds) Simply cut the cords or ribbons or ropes or chains which tie you to the people in the circle... (2 minutes) Do this gently and lovingly... (2 minutes) As you cut the cords, see the attachments simply dissolve away... (1 minute) Some may take longer than others... ...be patient... (2 minutes) The scissors will cut through, although this may take some time for some of the attachments... (2 minutes) Take as long as you need to sever each connection... (2 minutes) Check the circle again and make sure that all the attachments are completely removed... (1 minute) Now check the places where you have removed the ties, cords or attachments... (1 minute) These are the attachment points which you found on both yourself and the people you have been working with... (5 seconds) Bathe each attachment point with pink light. This light will cleanse, clear, heal and close each place where you have removed an attachment... (5 seconds) Do this for yourself, and for the other people too... (2 minutes) You have removed and healed the connections which bound you. You have released the negativity and so you can begin to heal these relationships... (20 seconds) Imagine a bubble of silver light forming in your own circle... (30 seconds) As you watch, the bubble grows taller and wider... (30 seconds) Until you are standing inside the bubble, completely surrounded by silver light... (1 minute) Now imagine a small bubble of silver light beginning to form in the second circle... (30 seconds) Watch as the second bubble of silver light grows taller and wider until everyone in the circle in front of you is standing inside the bubble of silver light... (1 minute) Now watch as your bubble of silver light sends a stream of healing silver light to everyone in the circle in front of you... (2 minutes) Everyone in the circle in front of you is now receiving healing silver light from you... (1 minute) You may speak to whoever is in the circle in front of you... (10 seconds) You may want to speak of unconditional love... (5 seconds) ...or forgiveness... (5 seconds) ...or understanding... (5 seconds) Take a few moments to say whatever you need to say... (2 minutes) Now thank each person in turn and ask them to leave the circle... (1—2 minutes) Watch them go... (15 seconds) When the circle in front of you is completely empty, just allow it to dissolve... (30 seconds) Still standing inside your circle surrounded by a bubble of silver light you may remain for as long as you need, taking the healing silver light for your own healing... (2—3 minutes) When you are ready, dissolve your bubble... (30 seconds) Check to make sure that the circle in front of you has completely disappeared... (15 seconds) Dissolve the circle in which you are standing... (30 seconds) And prepare to leave this healing inner journey... (20 seconds)

Close with chosen departure/grounding.

2. RELEASING AND HEALING CURRENT RELATIONSHIPS GUIDED MEDITATION

- To release and heal others who are currently involved in negative relationships with you (for example, partners, lovers, friends, children, parents, employers, colleagues, neighbours).
- Note: Like all the meditations, this meditation may

be repeated as many time as you like. So, you may prefer to deal with one relationship at a time or, you may prefer to work with a number of relationships at once. Before you begin the meditation, consider what feels right for you, and then follow your intuition. If you are unfamiliar with the chakra system, see chapter four for a full explanation of the chakras.

Switch on your tape-recorder; open with chosen introduction. Imagine you are standing in a clear space... (30 seconds) Draw a white circle on the ground around you... (10 seconds) You can use any substance to draw the circle, paint or light or something else of your own choosing... (30 seconds) Make sure the circle in which you are standing is completely closed and that you are standing in the centre... (1 minute) Now draw another circle, directly in front of your circle... (30 seconds) Make sure that the second circle does not touch or overlap the circle in which you are standing... (15 seconds) Now place inside the circle in front of you the person or people you wish to release and heal... (allow 1—2 minutes for each person) Begin by explaining to each person in turn how you feel about the current relationship... (30 seconds) Explain why you feel angry, or upset or betrayed or jealous or hurt... (3—4 minutes for each person) Now describe how you would like the relationship to be... (3—4 minutes for each person) Take this opportunity to tell each person that you like them, or love them or, at the very least, that you respect them... (1—2 minutes each person) Tell each person that you want to erase the negative energy which exists between you, and that you want to replace the negativity with Light and positive energy... (2 minutes) Now imagine that you are opening your crown chakra and ask for access to the highest source of Light which is available to you... (2 minutes) Draw down this golden light into your crown chakra... (1 minute) To the brow chakra... (30 seconds) To the throat chakra... (30 seconds) And finally to the heart chakra... (30 seconds) Allow this golden light to settle at your heart

45

chakra... (30 seconds) Feel the gentle healing energy... (2 minutes) Now gather this golden light and send it, from your chakra, to the heart chakra of each person in the circle in front of you... (3 minutes) Imagine this golden light filling and surrounding each person... (2 minutes) Until they are standing in a bubble of golden light... (1 minute) Golden light which is cleansing, clearing and healing all the negativity which exists between you... (30 seconds) Now, from your heart centre, send unconditional love to each person in the circle in front of you... (2 minutes) Let this unconditional love wash over them... (2 minutes) And allow the unconditional love to join with the golden light for their highest good... (2 minutes) When you are ready, begin to gently withdraw the golden light which you have been sending... (2 minutes) Allow the golden light to gather in front of you, do not take this back into your heart chakra... (1 minute) Instead send this golden light down into the earth at your feet... (1 minute) Now thank each person in turn and say goodbye... Watch as each person leaves the circle... (30 seconds) When the circle in front of you is completely empty allow it to dissolve... (30 seconds) Now focus your attention once more on your crown chakra and ask again for the highest source of Light which is available to you... (1 minute) Become aware of a pink light moving down through your crown chakra... (30 seconds) Into your brow... (30 seconds) Throat... (30 seconds) Heart... (30 seconds) Solar plexus... (30 seconds) Sacral... (30 seconds) And root... (30 seconds) Cleansing and clearing and healing... (30 seconds) When you are ready, gather this pink light and send it down, through your root chakra, into the earth .... (1 minute).. Check to make sure that the circle in front of you has completely disappeared... (15 seconds) Dissolve the circle in which you are standing... (30 seconds) You are now ready to return from this inner journey... (10 seconds)

Close with chosen departure/grounding.

3. Healing others who are physically ill or emotionally distressed

- To be used for the 'absent healing' of others.
- This guided meditation may be used for both people and animals.
- Note: by sending healing energy through the medium of a guided meditation you are, in effect, invading another person's 'personal space'.
  When working with people, I only ever use this meditation with the recipient's approval and agreement.

Switch on your tape-recorder; open with chosen introduction.

Imagine you are standing in a sacred space... (1 minute) You are inside a temple of healing... (1 minute) The air about you is fragrant with incense... (30 seconds) In the distance you can hear the faint sound of many voices blending in harmony, a healing and sacred chant, and all about you is peace and tranquillity... (1 minute) You are standing before a clear quartz crystal... (30 seconds) It is taller than you and much, much wider... (30 seconds) You reach out your hand and gently touch the surface... (30 seconds) It is cool to the touch and vibrating with energy... (30 seconds) A you watch, you see a section of the crystal open... (1 minute) There is a doorway wide enough for you to step inside... (30 seconds) You walk into the crystal and find that, inside, it is even more peaceful, more tranquil than the temple of healing... (1 minute) Stand for a moment and allow this wonderful peace and healing to pervade every part of your being... (1 minute) Now imagine that, standing in front of you, is the person you wish to heal... (1 minute) What are they wearing?... (30 seconds) How do they look?... (30 seconds) With your right hand reach out and touch the wall of the crystal... (30 seconds) As your hand makes the connection with the cool surface you can feel a current of healing energy moving into your fingertips... (1 minute) Reach out and, with your left hand, touch the solar plexus of the person you wish to heal... (30 seconds) You are the bridge between the healing energy of the crystal and the person you wish to heal... (30 seconds) Send the healing energy which you are receiving from the crystal, allowing the energy to travel from your right hand... (30 seconds) ...along your right arm... (30 seconds) ...into your solar plexus... (30 seconds) ...down your left arm... (30 seconds) ...to your left hand... (30 seconds) ...into the solar plexus of the person you wish to heal... (30 seconds) Maintain this connection for as long as you need to... (5 seconds) Either the other person will withdraw, or you will know when the healing is complete... (up to 10 minutes) When you are ready, remove your left hand from the person being healed, and remove your right hand from the crystal wall... (30 seconds) You may want to say something ... (5 seconds) Or the person who has received the healing may want to say something to you... (3 minutes) When you are ready, say good-bye... (30 seconds) ...and watch the other person leave. They may simply dissolve, or they may walk out of the crystal... (1 minute) Now you are alone in the crystal become aware of a healing gold and apricot light... (30 seconds) This light surrounds you... (1 minute) Cleanses you... (30 seconds) Revitalises you... (30 seconds) Take as much of the light as you need for your own healing and rejuvenation... (3 minutes) When you are ready the doorway in the crystal will slide open for you... (30 seconds) Step outside the crystal into the calm and peaceful healing temple... (30 seconds) On the floor, at your feet, a gift awaits you... (30 seconds) Pick it up and examine it. What is it?... (2 minutes) When you are ready, thank the unseen Guardians of the healing temple and prepare to leave this inner journey... (1 minute)

Close with chosen departure/grounding.

CHAPTER 4 — UNDERSTANDING YOUR CHAKRAS

One of the basic concepts of Eastern, and subsequently, New Age spiritual teachings, is that in addition to our physical, flesh and blood body we also have an 'energy' body, known as the aura. Until this century the existence of the aura was unproved although, then as now, many psychics were able to see and interpret the human aura.

In the early 1900s Dr W J Kilner began work at St Thomas' Hospital in London on an invention designed to show visibly, for the first time, ultra-violet light. As a result of his work he discovered accidentally that by using a specially designed screen, the human aura could be seen. As a result of his observations, Kilner developed a system for diagnosing illness and disease from examination of the aura. His book, *The Human Atmosphere*, which described his theories, was dismissed by the medical establishment.

Much later, in the 1960s, a Russian electrician, Semyon Kirlian, developed a camera capable of photographing the energy body, or aura, which surrounds all living things—humans, plants and animals.

Kirlian photographs, taken under rigidly controlled scientific conditions, were presented at the Soviet Scientific Conference in Russia in 1968. The photographs show that the aura combines with and extends beyond the physical body, and that it consists of coloured light and energy. The colours and strength of the aura vary from person to person, and the differences relate to the individual's physical, mental, emotional and spiritual condition.

The human aura extends between four to six inches (10 - 15 cm) beyond the body, appears even where a part of the physical body is missing (for instance if a limb has been amputated), and disappears completely once the body is clinically dead. In a person who is healthy, balanced and energised the aura colours will be strong and clear and bright. But someone who is suffering physical, mental, emotional or spiritual imbalance or illness will have an aura which contains dark, muddy colours, 'grey patches' or even 'holes' in the aura where no colours appear at all.

The human aura or energy field contains seven main energy centres which are called chakras, and it is the chakras which supply the colour and energy to the aura. Chakra is a Sanskrit word (Sanskrit being the ancient and sacred language of the Hindu religion), which means wheel. Those with the ability to see the chakras say that, within the aura, the chakras look like spinning wheels of coloured light. Hindu tradition describes the chakras as resembling the lotus flower; the chakra which functions at the highest vibratory rate at the crown of the head having the most petals, and the chakra which functions at the lowest vibratory rate (the root chakra, located between the legs), having the least petals.

In the same way that a healthy physical body depends on the effective functioning of major organs such as the heart, liver, kidneys, lungs, spleen and so on, a healthy aura depends on the effective functioning of the chakras. We are born with a complete chakra system and, at the time of birth, each of the seven chakras should be open and functioning.

Unfortunately, soon after arrival in the material world, the chakras may begin to close down or even shut-off completely. The higher chakras (crown, brow and throat), which are the bridge between the material and the spiritual worlds are usually the first to close. This is usually as a result of adult rejection of 'childish' ideas such as spirit friends, past life-recall, nature spirits and so on. We soon discover that by talking about such things we invite parental disapproval. Because children dislike ridicule and disbelief, we quickly learn to reject those 'fanciful concepts' which adults refuse to accept. We close our crown, brow and throat chakras, so that we will no longer be troubled by such 'daft ideas'. Moving down the aura, the heart chakra will also swiftly close as a result of physical or emotional abuse or rejection, or just plain and simple lack of love, understanding and approval.

When all seven chakras are balanced and working the aura or 'energy body' is strong and vibrant and we experience physical, mental, emotional and spiritual well-being. If the chakras become closed, blocked or imbalanced this affects the aura. Anything which affects the aura will have a consequent effect on the physical body, resulting in illness and disease. In the same way, mental, emotional and spiritual well-being and development are affected by the chakras.

It is for these reasons that most spiritual healing, which involves the channelling of energy from the healer to the subject, focuses on clearing, cleansing, balancing and energising the chakras and the aura. Whereas orthodox physicians concentrate on the physical organs, the blood, and so on, and homeopathic practitioners work with the 'vital force', healers who use channelled energy concentrate on the chakras and the aura. The basis of energy healing being that if the chakras are functioning effectively then everything else will follow. This makes sense if you think of the chakras as being the 'engine which drives the vehicle'.

Guided meditations are a useful technique to apply in order to ensure that each of the chakras are functioning properly. It is important to think of the seven chakras as a complete system. This means it is best not to concentrate solely on one or two, but instead work with each chakra in turn and regularly balance all seven together. To be balanced and functioning effectively, the chakras should be neither tightly closed, nor wide open.

The guided meditations which follow can be used in sequence to open, clear and balance each of the chakras in turn. It is interesting to note that there are seven major chakras and seven days of the week. I find it useful to work through the chakras on a daily basis, completing the week with the Crown Chakra Meditation and the Seven Chakra Meditation to balance the system. I also work through the Cording Meditation once a month or if I have had a particularly emotional or upsetting experience involving other people.

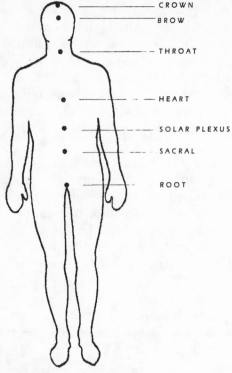

Fig.1 This illustration shows the placing of the chakras within your aura.

Root chakra

This is the first of the seven chakras. It is located within your aura between your legs in the genital area, and faces down to the earth.

The purpose of this chakra is to keep us connected to the earth and this physical, material world. A good way to ground yourself is to send a 'grounding cord' (imagine a rope or cord of energy and light), from your root chakra deep down into the earth. This is particularly useful either at the end of a guided meditation when you need to firmly anchor yourself back in this reality, or if you have been carrying out energy healing work or any other spiritual activity.

If your root chakra is out of balance or closed you may feel:

- 'spacey'   • 'up in the clouds'
- 'unreal'   • 'out of it'
- unable to deal with reality
- not connected with the 'here and now'

Anyone who is working with spiritual development should pay great attention to balancing their root chakra as this will provide a strong link back to the earth, this incarnation, this reality.

The colour which corresponds to the root chakra is red.

The sound which corresponds to the root chakra is *Oh*.

Before beginning your root chakra meditation you may like to take five or ten minutes to light a red candle and, sitting quietly with your spine straight and your body symmetrical, simply repeat the sound of *Oh*. This will help you to 'tune in' to your root chakra.

Root chakra guided meditation

Begin with your chosen introduction.

You find yourself in a forest... (30 seconds) Surrounded by ancient trees... (30 seconds) The tree trunks reach up to the sky, way above your head, and the branches interlock and create a protective canopy... (1 minute) The sunlight streams through the branches and the leaves, forming a pattern on the earth beneath your feet... (30 seconds) As you walk the soles of your feet connect with the rich, dark soil... (30 seconds) You can smell the earth... (30 seconds) You notice the leaves on the branches above your head and you see the colours... (30 seconds) ...green and gold and russet and amber... (30 seconds) As you walk further and deeper into the forest you come to a particular tree, ancient and proud, very tall and very strong... (30 seconds) And you know that you are welcome in this space and that the tree wishes to act as a bridge for you, a connection between your energy and earth energy... (30 seconds) At the base of the tree the roots extend in all directions in a complex web which reaches deep into the ground... (30 seconds) There is a space for you among the roots. A space which has been created to fit you exactly... (10 seconds) Sit down, make yourself comfortable... (30 seconds) Be aware now that the tree is cradling you, gently but firmly protecting and guarding you, ensuring that no harm can come to you... (30 seconds) As you lean back again the bark of this ancient tree trunk you sense the energy and life force within... (1 minute) And your feet, firm against the rich, brown earth, sense the energy within the earth... (1 minute) The sunlight streaming through the canopy of branches and leaves above your head change from yellow to orange to a warm, deep rose-pink... (30 seconds) You are bathed in a pool of healing rose-tinted light... (1 minute) You become aware that the tree is breathing too... (1 minute) And as you breathe in the healing rose light you are channelling this light to the tree... (2 minutes) And the tree is sending the light deep down to the core of the earth... (2 minutes) To nurture and to heal the earth... (30 seconds) And as the tree breathes out you receive healing energy from deep within the earth... (2 minutes) You feel the connection, the circle of nurturing and healing between the rose-tinted light and yourself and the tree and the earth... (30 seconds) You are at one with the earth... (2 minutes) You are healing the earth... (2 minutes) You are being healed by the earth... (2 minutes) Remain here for a while, giving to the earth, and taking from the earth... (3 minutes) Slowly the rose-pink light begins to change to amber... (30 seconds) Then to a clear golden yellow... (30 seconds) You know it is time to leave... (30 seconds) Still sitting, cradled within the roots of the tree, become aware of your root chakra, which is now cleansed and cleared... (1 minute) You may decide to leave this chakra wide open, or you may prefer to close it slightly... (1 minute)

But make sure that you retain the connection between your root chakra and the earth's energy... (1 minute) You say farewell to the tree... (1 minute) Knowing that you will return when you choose to, when the time is right ....(30 seconds) Now begin to re-trace your steps back along your original path... (30 seconds) Back to the place where this healing journey began... (30 seconds)
End with your chosen departure/grounding.

SACRAL CHAKRA

This is the second chakra in the chakra system, and it is located just below the navel.

This is the chakra which enables us to be sensitive to other people's emotions, and to sense dangerous or emotionally-charged situations. Sometimes this can be useful but, if your sacral chakra is wide-open, it can mean that you take on other people's emotions and feelings. For instance, if you spend time with someone who is upset or depressed and they leave you feeling fine, whilst you feel emotionally 'churned-up', the chances are that your sacral chakra is wide-open and you have absorbed their negative energies into your own aura.

If you sacral chakra is wide-open you may feel:
• 'drained' by contact with other people
• emotionally charged by other people's problems, even though they are nothing to do with you
• constantly aware of 'atmospheres' and 'tensions' which others seem unaware of.

Anyone who works with others as, for example, a teacher, counsellor, or healer, should pay particular attention to the sacral chakra, as this will help you to protect yourself from others' emotions and problems. The sacral chakra is also connected with sex and sexuality so, if you need to heal traumas connected with sexuality, particularly difficulties which stem from childhood, then work on this chakra will help to heal 'old wounds'. Someone with a sacral chakra which is either wide open or tightly closed, will have corresponding sexual attitudes or behaviour. Any work done to balance the sacral will have a complementary effect on the physical circumstances and condition.

The colour which corresponds to the sacral chakra is orange.

The sound which corresponds to the sacral chakra is *Oo* (as in shoe or few).

Before beginning your sacral chakra meditation you may like to take five or ten minutes to light an orange candle and, sitting quietly with your spine straight and your body symmetrical, simply repeat the sound of *Oo*. This will help you to 'tune in' to your sacral chakra.

SACRAL CHAKRA GUIDED MEDITATION

Begin with your chosen introduction.

You are walking up a narrow path... (30 seconds) On either side of the path there is green grass, and set here and there, amidst the grass, are small, wild flowers of every colour and shape... (30 seconds) The air is clear and fresh and the sky above is blue... (30 seconds) As you reach the brow of the hill you see a small white building... (1 minute) Make your way towards it... (30 seconds) You see in front of the building two Guardians... (30 seconds) They are waiting for you and they know that their task is to protect and guard you whilst you are inside the building... (30 seconds) As you move closer you can see that the Guardians are bathed in golden light... (1 minute) They smile in welcome as you approach... (30 seconds) A small door set into the side of the white building swings open... (30 seconds) You enter... (30 seconds) Inside the building it is cool and the light is soft... (1 minute) There is only one room and in the centre of the room there is a seat of white marble... (30 seconds) You sit down, finding that the marble seat is surprisingly comfortable... (30 seconds) From a point just above your head you see that the room begins to fill with a warm apricot light... (1 minute) The light surrounds you... (1

56

minute) Floods every fibre of your being, bringing gentle warmth and healing... (1 minute) You feel a lightness and a radiance throughout your body... (1 minute) The warm apricot light is flushing away all negativity... (30 seconds) Negativity which has been generated by you, and negativity which you may have gathered and absorbed from your contact with other people... (30 seconds) Every fibre of your physical body is cleansed and renewed... (1 minute) Your aura is cleansed and cleared throughout... (30 seconds) Feel the apricot light gently streaming down on your sacral chakra Gently washing the chakra with pure, healing light... (3 minutes) Take as much of the light as you need, until you feel renewed and revitalised... (4 minutes) Now you know that you are now carrying and holding only your own, pure energies... (30 seconds) Now it is time to leave this room, knowing that you can return to this cleansing light whenever you choose... (30 seconds) Close the door behind you... (30 seconds) Say farewell to the two Guardians who will remain here to keep this place safe for you until you return... (1 minute) Walk back down the narrow path bordered by grass on either side... (30 seconds) Until you find yourself at the place where your healing journey began... (30 seconds)

End with your chosen departure/grounding.

SOLAR PLEXUS CHAKRA

This is the third of the seven chakras. It is located within your aura at the site of the solar plexus, which is just slightly below the breast bone.

The solar plexus chakra is the aura's psychic energy centre. Because everything which happens in the aura has a consequent effect on the physical body, too much activity in the this chakra can result in anxiety, nervous tension, 'stomach-churning' and so on, at the physical level.

If your solar plexus chakra is wide-open you may:
- feel anxious, nervous, 'jumpy & jittery', startled at the least sound

- be adversely aware of psychic activity, either current or from past events

Also, anyone who works with their psychic senses, for example as a spirit channel or as a card 'reader' should pay particular attention to the condition of the solar plexus chakra and should always make sure that this centre is partially closed on completion of any psychic work.

The colour which corresponds to the solar plexus chakra is yellow.

The sound which corresponds to the solar plexus chakra is *Ah* (as in car or far).

Before beginning your solar plexus chakra meditation you may like to take five or ten minutes to light a yellow candle and, sitting quietly with your spine straight and your body symmetrical, simply repeat the sound of *Ah*. This will help you to 'tune in' to your solar plexus chakra.

Solar plexus chakra guided meditation

Begin with your chosen introduction.

It is dawn and you are walking on the beach... (30 seconds) The fine, white sand beneath your feet is cool and comfortable... (30 seconds) The only sound is the gentle roar of the ocean as the waves break on the shore... (1 minute) The clean white foam bubbles across the sand towards you... (30 seconds) You walk to the water's edge and allow the incoming waves to ebb around your ankles... (1 minute). On the horizon the sun is rising, casting swathes of lemon and gold and rose across the pale sky... (30 seconds) You sit on the sand... (1 minute) Dip your toes in the warm, salty ocean... (1 minute) You hear a faint sound, little more than an echo on the wind... (30 seconds) You see a dolphin swimming towards you, leaping and arcing out of the water to attract your attention... (1 minute) You wait patiently, watching him approach... (1 minute) Then right beside you is this great creature, and in his mouth is a crystal...

(30 seconds) Carried through the waves as a gift for you... (30 seconds) He drops the crystal, a golden citrine, in your lap... (30 seconds) You examine the crystal and as the sun rises higher, the sky is filled with a beautiful yellow light which is reflected in the citrine which you hold in your hand... (1 minute) The dolphin lays his head in your lap and looks up at you... (30 seconds) Your eyes meet and you sense his intelligence and joy in life... (1 minute) You may ask him if he has a message for you. If he does, listen carefully, for whatever he has to say will be important... (3 minutes) Now it is time for him to leave. Thank him for the gift of the crystal and watch as he slips into the water and swims away... (2 minutes) Lift the citrine in both hands and gently place it against your sacral chakra... (30 seconds) You can feel the golden light and the gentle vibration of this stone cleansing, clearing and balancing your solar plexus chakra... (2 minutes) Take as much of the light and vibration as you need... (3 minutes) Accept the crystal healing and know that your strength and courage and power have been renewed... (30 seconds) Now, feeling calm and peaceful, you can choose to either leave the citrine or to bring it with you... (1 minute) Say farewell, once more, to your dolphin, who is now swimming far beyond the seashore... (1 minute) Take one last look at the ocean... (30 seconds) And the sun, now high overhead... (30 seconds) Knowing that you can return to this beach at any time you choose... (30 seconds) And begin to retrace your steps along the beach to the place where this healing journey began... (30 seconds)

End with your chosen departure/grounding.

HEART CHAKRA

This the fourth chakra in the system and is located at the same level as your physical heart, but is directly in the centre of the chest.

This chakra is connected with the emotions and with the feelings of love, tenderness and compassion for other individuals, groups, yourself and the Source or, if you prefer, God.

Difficulties with relationships often stem from an imbalance in this chakra and certainly anyone who experiences difficulty with self-confidence, self-esteem, self-forgiveness and self-love needs to cleanse, clear and open this centre.

If your heart chakra is closed you may feel:
- isolated and cut off from love, tenderness, compassion and understanding.
- unable to love or care for others.
- unlovable, and undeserving of care and attention from others.
- insecure and jealous.

If your heart chakra is wide open you may:
- give of yourself to others to such an extent that there is nothing left for you.

Anyone who has suffered emotional difficulties in childhood, stemming from parental rejection, will most likely have a closed heart chakra.

Each subsequent rejection offered by friends, lovers, partners will affect this chakra. A properly functioning, well-balanced heart chakra will enable you to give and accept love, and create loving relationships.

The colours which corresponds to the heart chakra are rose-pink and green. The sound which corresponds to the heart chakra is *Ay* (as in say or way).

Before beginning your heart chakra meditation you may like to take five or ten minutes to light a pink or green candle and, sitting quietly with your spine straight and your body symmetrical, simply repeat the sound of *Ay*. This will help you to 'tune in' to your heart chakra.

Begin with your chosen introduction.

You find yourself standing in front of a small wooden door... (1 minute) Gently push the door and you will see that it swings open... (30 seconds). Through the open door you catch the fragrance of roses... (30 seconds) Step through the door and find yourself in a rose garden... (30 seconds) All around you, and as far as you can see, there are roses of every shape and type and colour. There are rosebuds and fully open blooms of pink and lemon and white and apricot and red and gold and lilac and cream... (2 minutes) You see that there are a number of pathways which lead to the centre of the rose garden... (30 seconds) Choose the path you wish to take... (1 minute) Walk the path, bordered on either side by a profusion of roses... (20 seconds) The heady fragrance of roses fills the air all around you, and the sun shines down from a clear blue sky... (2 minutes) At last you reach the centre of the garden and there you find a very unusual, very special rose bush... (30 seconds) On this very special rose bush there are roses of every colour and size imaginable... (1 minute) Consider the bush and choose your rose... (1 minute) What colour is it?... (30 seconds) Is it a bud or a full-grown bloom?... (30 seconds).. The petals of your rose open slightly and you bend forward to breathe in the perfume... (30 seconds) Bending over the rose you see at the heart of the flower a small rose-quartz crystal... (30 seconds) The rose quartz glows with a soft rosy-pink light... (30 seconds) Gently you place your fingertips on the crystal... (30 seconds) You feel the warm healing vibrations of the crystal slowly moving through your fingertips... (1 minute) Along your arm... (30 seconds) Into your heart chakra... (30 seconds) The rose-pink light expands, spreads out beyond your heart chakra, bathing your entire physical body and energy aura in a rosy glow... (2 minutes) You experience a sense of complete inner peace... (2 minutes) Aware that everything in your life is unfolding as it should... (1 minute) Now focus your attention on your heart chakra... (30 seconds) Notice whether it is closed tightly or wide open... (30 seconds) How should it be?... (30 seconds) How would you like it to be?... (30 seconds) Does it need to be a little more open?... (30 seconds) A little more closed?... (30 seconds) Concentrante on balancing your heart chakra... (4 minutes) When you are satisfied that your heart chakra is how you would like it to be, return your attention to the rose quartz crystal which is still in the centre of your rose... (1 minute) Feel the unconditional love which is pouring from this crystal... (30 seconds) Unconditional love which is being absorbed by every fibre of your being... (1 minute) Take as much of this love as you need to heal old hurts and wounds... (3 minutes) Decide now whether you wish to leave the rose-quartz in the rose or whether you wish to remove it and bring it with you... (1 minute) Now it is time to leave... (30 seconds) Turning, you begin to retrace your steps, walking back from the centre of the peaceful garden... (30 seconds) Along the path, past the roses... (30 seconds) Knowing this garden will always be here for you, whenever you wish to return... (30 seconds) Back through the small wooden door... (30 seconds) To the place where this healing journey began... (30 seconds) End with your chosen departure/grounding.

THROAT CHAKRA

This is the fifth chakra and is located in the aura at the throat, just at the base of the larynx.

This is the chakra of communication. The communication you send to and receive from others and, most importantly, the communication you receive from your inner Wise One who knows everything and who is available to give you appropriate advice whenever it is needed.

When your throat chakra is closed you may:
- experience difficulty in communicating verbally. This could mean that you have difficulty with expressing your emotions and with asking for what you want and saying what you need.

- find that the imbalance present in this chakra manifests itself in the physical body as illnesses such as a recurring sore throat, laryngitis, nervous cough, 'lump in the throat'.

If you are working to develop your ability to access your inner wisdom, then you should pay particular attention to the throat chakra, as this will facilitate the flow of inner communication.

The colour which corresponds to the throat chakra is blue.

The sound which corresponds to the throat chakra is *Ee* (as in see or tea).

Before beginning your throat chakra meditation you may like to take five or ten minutes to light a blue candle and, sitting quietly with your spine straight and your body symmetrical, simply repeat the sound of *Ee*. This will help you to 'tune in' to your throat chakra.

THROAT CHAKRA GUIDED MEDITATION

Begin with your chosen introduction.

You find yourself in an open boat, gently drifting on a calm sea.. (1 minute) There is a light breeze... (30 seconds) Birds fly overhead, their calls echoing over the sparkling water... (30 seconds) The rhythm of the boat on the waves rocks you gently... (30 seconds) You are completely relaxed and at ease... (1 minute) In the distance you see a small island, a patch of green surrounded by blue water... (1 minute) The boat gently drifts towards the island... (1 minute) The boats runs aground on the sand and you leave the vessel, stepping lightly ashore, knowing that the boat will wait for you... (1 minute) Walk up the beach and towards trees and flowers... (1 minute) Entering a clearing you see in front of you, in the centre, a magical tree hung with silver bells... (1 minute) The branches spread out like a canopy and every branch is hung with a silver filigree of bells of every shape and size... (30 seconds) The tree is quite small and you can easily reach the bells where they cascade down from the branches... (30 seconds) Consider the bells... (30 seconds) Which one is yours?... (30 seconds) Reach forward and touch your special bell... (1 minute) There is clear, pure, silvery sound which echoes around the clearing... (1 minute) You recognise that this is a special healing sound created just for you... (30 seconds) The sound swells and blends into a harmony... (2 minutes) A magical chord which is cleansing and balancing your throat chakra... (30 seconds) The sound washes over you and you sing it back to the tree... (2 minutes) And as you make the sound you know that you are clearing and opening your throat chakra... (30 seconds) That this is your very own special healing sound... (30 seconds) Allow the sound to wash over you until you feel that your throat chakra is completely cleansed and balanced... (3 minutes) When you are ready, leave the clearing... (1 minute) Knowing that you may return here to this magical place whenever you wish... (30 seconds) Retrace your steps back down the beach to the seashore where your boat is waiting for you... (30 seconds) Step inside and allow the boat to gently drift out to sea, carried by the slow-moving current... (30 seconds) Gently, slowly, the boat returns you to the place where this healing journey began... (1 minute).

End with your chosen departure/grounding.

Brow chakra

This is the sixth chakra and is located in the aura just above and between the eyebrows.

The brow chakra is the chakra of intuition and of clairvoyance (which means clear-seeing), and is connected with both outer and inner seeing. Your ability to visualise, to create 'mental pictures' and to manifest into reality that which you create mentally, are all connected with the brow chakra.

Quite often there is strong 'tension' between the harsh realities and practicalities of day-to-day living and the gentler aspects of spiritual life.

When your brow chakra is closed you may:

- feel that you are 'out of place' in this day-to-day existence.
- be aware that 'there is more to life' or seek to understand 'why you are here.'

If you would like to develop your intuition, or your ability to visualise, then it is particularly important to ensure that your brow chakra is balanced and functioning clearly.

The colour which corresponds to the brow chakra is indigo.

The sound which corresponds to the brow chakra is *Om* (as in Tom or from).

Before beginning your brow chakra meditation you may like to take five or ten minutes to light a dark blue, turquoise or amethyst candle and, sitting quietly with your spine straight and your body symmetrical, simply repeat the sound of *Om*. This will help you to 'tune in' to your brow chakra.

BROW CHAKRA MEDITATION

Begin with your chosen introduction.

You find yourself on a hillside... (30 seconds) It is early morning and the air is crisp and clear... (30 seconds) Walk up the slight incline, towards the brow of the hill... (1 minute) As you reach the summit you see an eagle waiting for you... (30 seconds) As you walk towards this majestic bird he spreads his wings in greeting... (1 minute) On his back is a small enclosed seat... (30 seconds) Climb into the seat and, using the silver cords you find, carefully strap yourself in... (1 minute) The eagle turns his head and for a moment there is a wordless communication between the two of you ... (1 minute) You know that you will be safe... (30 seconds) At your word the eagle takes to the sky... (1 minute) You feel the gentle air currents flow past your face and hair... (1 minute) Below, you see the green earth and the silver sea... (30 seconds) You fly over mountains, rivers, valleys, forests, deserts, lakes, canyons... (1 minute) Until below you see a mountain, capped with snow, and you know that is your destination... (30 seconds) The eagle soars in, adjusting his speed... (1 minute) Lands carefully and gently... (30 seconds) You untie the silver cords which have held you and dismount, knowing that the eagle will wait for you... (1 minute) Begin to walk the short distance to the mountain peak... (30 seconds) Look around you, notice the tiny flowers and grasses growing amongst the snow... (30 seconds) See the ancient rocks and boulders... (30 seconds) The stars above... (30 seconds) The indigo blue sky... (1 minute) At the peak of the mountain you find a cloak. It is made of the softest wool, and its colour is the deep blue of the night sky... (30 seconds) Wrap yourself in this cloak... (30 seconds) And as the folds of the cloak drape around you, be aware of a perfect stillness, a perfect peace... (1 minute) Focus now on your brow chakra... (30 seconds) Raise your face to the moon and allow the gentle, healing rays of the moon to cleanse and balance your brow chakra... (2 minutes) Enfolded in your cloak, bathed in moonlight, you are at peace... (2 minutes) Sit under the healing rays of the moon until you can feel that your brow chakra is completely balanced... (4 minutes) When you are ready, slip off the indigo cloak and lay it gently on the ground... (30 seconds) Make your way to where the eagle awaits you... (1 minute) Climb aboard and tie the silver cords... (30 seconds) The eagle arcs into the air, spreading his great wings and soars out over the landscape once again... (30 seconds) The wind is in your hair, the moon and stars guide you back... (2 minutes) The eagle begins his descent, swooping down to land... (1 minute) Untie the silver cords and say farewell, knowing that you may return to travel with the eagle whenever you choose... (30 seconds) You are now, once again, back where this

inner journey began... (30 seconds)
End with your chosen departure/grounding.

CROWN CHAKRA

This is the seventh and final chakra in the seven chakra system, and is located in the aura at the top or 'crown' of the head. This chakra connects with the Higher Realms and is the 'gateway' to the astral planes and higher levels of consciousness. When the crown chakra is open and functioning effectively we are able to access our Higher Selves and a higher level of guidance than that provided by our own inner Wise One. A well-balanced crown chakra will help your spiritual development and your ability to operate comfortably both in the here-and-now of the material world, and in your journey along the spiritual path.

If your crown chakra is closed you may feel:
- 'cut-off' from your Higher Self.
- frustrated or confused with regard to your inner spiritual life.
- conscious that there is 'more to life than this' but feeling unable to access those higher energies.

Anyone who is walking the path of spiritual development should pay particular attention to this chakra, as an open, well-balanced and receptive crown chakra will help you to access the highest energies available to you.

The colours which corresponds to the crown chakra are violet, silver and gold.

The sound which corresponds to the brow chakra is *Ing* (as in ring or sing)

Before beginning your crown chakra meditation you may like to take five or ten minutes to light a violet, silver or gold candle and, sitting quietly with your spine straight and your body symmetrical, simply repeat the sound of *Ing*. This will help you to 'tune in' to your crown chakra.

Open with your chosen introduction.

You are standing on a mountain top... (30 seconds) The star-filled sky is above you, and all around you are snow crystals, sparkling like diamonds... (1 minute) The moon casts a gentle light, watching over and protecting you... (1 minute) The night air is crisp and clear and you can see for miles... (30 seconds) The moonlit landscape stretches out below you... (1 minute).. Rivers and forests and streams and meadows... (30 seconds) Your name is called softly and gently, and turning, you see your Guide... (1 minute) A Being of Light who knows everything there is to know about you, and who accepts you completely and offers you unlimited unconditional love... (1 minute) As you walk towards your Guide your whole being is filled with light and energy... (2 minutes) Your Guide is holding a small bowl and within the bowl burns a violet flame... (30 seconds) Accept the bowl from your Guide and gaze into the violet flame... (1 minute) Now your Guide stands behind you and places his or her hands upon your shoulders... (30 seconds) At the contact you feel the love and the healing energy pour through your body... (2 minutes) You are aware that the violet flame is accepting and releasing all the negative energy and negative vibrations you have been carrying and holding... (3 minutes) As you watch the violet flame you feel that you are as one with the flame... (2 minutes) And you are aware of the current of healing energy which is passing from your Guide to you... (2 minutes) Clearing and cleansing, healing and renewing... (30 seconds) You are aware of a deep sense of inner peace and serenity... (2 minutes) You feel your Guide gently touch the crown of your head and you know that your crown chakra is being balanced and opened... (2 minutes) You may have a question for your Guide... Or you may want to say something to your Guide... (2 minutes) Listen carefully to the response... (3 minutes) Gently your Guide takes the bowl from your hands... (30 seconds) And you watch as this shimmering Being of Light waves farewell, turns

and begins to walk down the mountain... (1 minute) You know this mountain and your Guide are now always available to you, whenever you choose to return... (1 minute) Take one last look around, at the velvet sky, the twinkling stars, the moonlit landscape... (1 minute) And prepare to leave this inner journey... (30 seconds)
Close with chosen departure/grounding.

THE SEVEN CHAKRA SYSTEM

It really is most important not to pay too much attention to only one or two of the chakras, to the exclusion of the others. The chakras are a system of seven energy centres which work together to maintain physical, emotional and spiritual health in the same way that the heart, lungs, kidneys, liver and blood work together to maintain a healthy body. Having worked through the system, paying equal individual attention to the root, sacral, solar plexus, heart, throat, brow and crown, it is wise to give some time to balancing the complete system.

SEVEN CHAKRA GUIDED MEDITATION

Switch on your tape-recorder; open with chosen introduction.

Now that you are completely relaxed, begin by asking for access to the highest source of Light which is available to you... (2 minutes) Focus on your crown chakra and imagine a centre of spinning violet energy and light... (2 minutes) Allow your crown chakra to open like the petals of a flower... (1 minute) Move to your brow chakra and imagine a centre of spinning indigo energy and light... (2 minutes) Allow your brow chakra to open like the petals of a flower... (1 minute) Focus now on your throat chakra and imagine a centre of spinning blue energy and light... (2 minutes) Allow your throat chakra to open like the petals of a flower... (1 minute) Move down to your heart chakra and imagine a centre of spinning pink energy and light... (2 minutes) Allow your heart chakra to open like the petals of a flower... (1 minute) Now pay attention to your solar plexus and

69

imagine a centre of spinning yellow energy and light... (2 minutes) Allow your solar plexus chakra to open like the petals of a flower... (1 minute) Move now to your sacral chakra and imagine a centre of spinning orange energy and light... (2 minutes) Allow your sacral chakra to open like the petals of a flower... (1 minute) And moving down to the root chakra imagine a centre of spinning red energy and light... (2 minutes) Allow your root chakra to open like the petals of a flower... (1 minute) Become aware again of your crown chakra and draw down, through your crown, the highest source of Light which is available to you... (2 minutes) Feel this golden light move down through the chakras... (30 seconds) Through the crown, to the brow... (30 seconds) The throat, the heart... (30 seconds) The solar plexus, the sacral... (30 seconds) The root... (30 seconds) And then back up from the root to the sacral, the solar plexus... (30 seconds) To the heart... (30 seconds) Allow this gentle, golden, healing energy to settle at your heart centre... (2 minutes) Check each of your chakras in turn, crown, brow, throat, heart, solar plexus, sacral and root... (1 minute) Is each centre spinning in the same direction as the other centres?... (30 seconds) Does any centre seem 'tired' or closed?... (30 seconds) As you check, if you see a chakra which needs restoring, send the golden light to it... (30 seconds) Allow the golden light to give healing and energy to whichever chakras need attention... (3 minutes) When you are satisfied that each chakra is spinning freely focus once more on the golden light at your heart centre... (1 minute) Gather the golden light and send it downwards through your solar plexus, sacral and root... (1 minute) Deep into the earth, to heal and energise... (30 seconds) Now working upwards from the root, check each chakra to make sure that it is neither wide-open nor tightly closed. Aim for an energy centre which is spinning freely, mid-way open and receptive... (10 seconds) Work through the sacral... (30 seconds) The solar plexus... (30 seconds). The heart... (30 seconds) The throat... (30 seconds). The brow... (30 seconds). The

crown... (30 seconds) You are now ready to end this healing inner journey... (30 seconds)
Close with chosen departure/grounding.

CLEARING CHAKRA CORDS

Every time we connect with other people we exchange
emotions and energies. This happens between people who
are closely involved—friends, lovers, counsellors, teachers
and so on—and also between people who barely know each
other. The Traffic Warden and the Ticket Recipient; the
Doctor and the Patient; the Harassed Check-out Operator
and the Equally Harassed Shopper! Whenever we interact
with another person there is an energy exchange.
Sometimes this exchange can be obviously 'highly-charged'
on the physical level—for example, if you 'disagree' with
another motorist over a parking space or if you 'disagree'
with your partner over the washing-up. Sometimes,
though, the exchange of energy operates on a more subtle
level, and we are not even aware of the other person's emotional 'temperature'. For example, if someone you know
only slightly desires you sexually, or if someone at work
regards you as a rival, or if your child's teacher views you as
an over-indulgent parent, all of these types of situations
can lead to chakra cording. This simply means that someone has sent a line of energy to you which has become
embedded in one or other of your chakras. This happens
when people are sexually attracted to you, when they want
something from you or they want to give something to you.
It is worth noting that you will have sent lines of energy to
other people and, in the same way that you were unaware
of what you were doing, other people will have hooked
themselves into you without realising what they were doing.

Although you can safely remain connected to other people's energy for the rest of your life without coming to any
harm whatsoever, it is a good idea to check your chakras
for cording from time to time. By doing this on a fairly regular basis (say once a month), you can ensure that you are
operating from your own energy alone, and that your
chakras are clear and balanced.

Switch on your tape-recorder; open with chosen introduction.

Begin by looking at your root chakra... (30 seconds) Can you see any cords attached to this energy centre?... (30 seconds) A cord may be thick or thin, strong or fragile any of any colour. It may look like a thin stream of energy... (30 seconds) ...or a thick cord of rope... (30 seconds) If you find any cords attached to your root chakra imagine your own hands gently easing the cord away from your chakra. Be very gentle. Most cords will slide out when you want to remove them. If you have any difficulties simply ask the cord who owns it. And then follow the cord from your chakra until you see or feel or sense the person to whom it belongs. Gently explain to the cord's owner that you no longer wish to be attached... (2 minutes) Return to your own chakra and ease the cord away. If the cord will not slide out be aware that this is because you do not wish to lose the cord... (30 seconds) When your root chakra is cleared, visualise a stream of rose-pink light gently washing this energy centre. Cleansing, clearing, healing and balancing... (1 minute) Now move to your sacral chakra. Gently remove any cords you find there,... (1 minute) Now gently bathe the sacral chakra in a stream of pale orange light... (2 minutes) Watch as the chakra is cleansed, cleared, healed and balanced... (30 seconds) Move to the solar plexus. Are you aware of any cords?... (30 seconds) If so, gently remove them... (30 seconds) Then wash the solar plexus chakra with pale yellow light... (2 minutes) Cleansing, clearing, healing and balancing... (30 seconds) Move now to the heart chakra. Gently remove any cords your find and bathe the heart chakra with a stream of green light... (3 minutes) Observe as the heart chakra is cleansed, cleared, healed and balanced... (30 seconds) Go now to your throat chakra and check for cords. Gently remove them... (30 seconds) And send a cool stream of blue light to cleanse, clear, heal and balance... (2 minutes) Move up to the brow chakra and if you find any cords gently ease them away... (1 minute) Wash the brow chakra with a stream of blue light to cleanse, clear, heal and balance... (2 minutes) Go up to the brow chakra. Gently remove any cords you may find... (30 seconds) Then bathe this chakra with a stream of indigo light... (2 minutes) Watch as the brow chakra is cleansed, cleared, healed and balanced... (30 seconds) Finally go to your crown chakra. If you find any cords here, gently remove them... (30 seconds) Send a stream of golden light to your crown chakra to cleanse, clear, heal and balance... (3 minutes) Now return to your root and work your way through the system... (30 seconds) Root, sacral, solar plexus, heart, throat, brow and crown, checking that each chakra is spinning freely, mid-way open and receptive... (2 minutes) You are now ready to end this inner journey... (1 minute)

Close with your chosen departure/grounding

CHAPTER 5—
WORKING WITH THE TAROT

Be afraid of nothing
You have within you
All wisdom
All power
All strength
All understanding

Eileen Caddy*

HISTORY OF THE CARDS

The origins of the tarot are shrouded in mystery and conjecture because no-one really knows, for sure, where the cards come from. A widely accepted history is that the tarot originated in Egypt and was the sacred teaching of the Egyptian god of wisdom, Thoth. In fact, the tarot pack devised by Aleister Crowley is called The Book of Thoth. It is thought that in order to preserve these teachings, the tarot was entrusted to the Gypsies, who brought the wisdom out of Egypt and then dispersed to the Indian subcontinent, taking the tarot with them. (It is worth noting the striking similarity between the words Egypt and Gypsy.)

It is commonly held that whilst the Gypsies were guardians of the tarot (at any time during the period 5000 BC to 641 AD), the tarot was not presented in the form of playing cards, but was most likely to have been a book of some kind. One hypothesis is that this special knowledge was eventually transferred onto playing cards in the hope that people would use the cards for games of chance and wager without realising the importance of the images. It was hoped that by this means the knowledge would be pre-

*The Dawn of Change, Findhorn Press, 1979

served, but only certain people would have the necessary knowledge to access the true meaning of the cards.

The first recorded reference to the tarot was made in an Italian manuscript which dates from 1500 and, since that time, the tarot has been the subject of much speculation, discussion and, in some cases, heated argument.

COMPOSITION OF THE PACK

Each complete tarot deck consists of seventy-eight cards which are divided into the Major Arcana, which means Greater Secrets, and Lesser Arcana, which means Lesser Secrets.

There are twenty-two Major Arcana cards (which are also sometimes called Trumps, Keys or Atouts), each of which bears a powerful image. These are: Fool, Magician, High Priestess, Empress, Emperor, Hierophant, Lovers, Chariot, Justice, Hermit, Wheel of Fortune, Strength, Hanged Man, Death, Temperance, Devil, Tower, Star, Moon, Sun, Judgement, The World. The Major Arcana cards are considered to be the most powerful when they appear in a tarot reading. This is because they relate to the wider issues of 'who we are and why we are here'.

There are also fifty-six Minor Arcana cards, which are separated into four suits, in the same way that ordinary playing cards are divided into suits. The correspondences between the tarot and ordinary playing cards are:

Tarot	*wands*	correspond to playing card	*clubs*
Tarot	*coins*	correspond to playing card	*diamonds*
Tarot	*cups*	correspond to playing card	*hearts*
Tarot	*swords*	correspond to playing card	*spades*

The Lesser Arcana relates to the more mundane realms of:
- Business & enterprise   *wands*   element: fire
- Money   *coins*   element: earth
- Relationships & matters of the heart   *cups*   element: water
- Thought/mental energy   *swords*   element: air

In a tarot reading, Lesser Arcana cards are taken to refer to the practical, day-to-day issues of jobs, money, love affairs, health and so on.

Each of the four tarot suits of wands, coins, cups and swords consists of ten number cards, (Ace to Ten), plus four court cards (King, Queen, Knight and Page). Tarot packs vary enormously and some tarot designers have chosen to include the addition of a Princess in each of the suits.

Using the tarot

Some sources say the twenty-two cards of the Major Arcana contain Universal Wisdom of the highest order, some say the cards represent our journey through life, and some prefer Jung's* interpretation that each card represents an 'archetype', a universal symbol which has significance for everyone, throughout the world. This means that, for example the image of, say, a Warrior or a Crone or a Teacher, presented through a picture, a poem, a song or a story can be recognised and understood equally well by a financier in the City of London and a tribesman in the Brazilian jungle.

Much superstition surrounds the cards which, in themselves, have no power. They neither invite 'good' or 'bad' luck and they cannot 'make things happen'. A tarot card reader will interpret the images drawn by the querent and can explain the events which the tarot suggests are most likely to happen if the querent continues with his or her current thought-patterns/emotional responses/life-style. Because we have free will and can change the way we think and respond, we can change the outcome of any situation. So, a tarot reading will not describe events which will happen, it will merely indicate a path of future possibilities based on current events and responses.

The tarot is a rich source of imagery for guided meditations as the cards can help you to access your inner Wise One. The tarot designs undoubtedly appeal to the right

*Carl Gustav Jung, 1875-1961. Swiss psychiatrist, contemporary of Sigmund Freud, whose work centred on the theory of the 'archetypal unconscious' which postulates that there is a pool of ideas which is shared universally.

side of the brain which is intuitive, psychic, feminine and emotional, rather than the left side of the brain which is rational, logical, analytical and masculine.

Choosing a tarot pack to work with

Tarot packs have undergone many changes in design since first being used as playing cards in the 1370s. Nowadays it is possible to buy a wide selection of different types of decks and, if you decide to work with the tarot for guided meditations, it is best to simply choose the pack which you find most pleasing. There isn't a 'right' or 'wrong' pack to use. Just select the pack to which you respond best, maybe because you prefer the colours, the designs or even the size or shape of the cards. If you feel happy and comfortable with the cards you have chosen, then that is the right pack for you.

When to use tarot card
guided meditations

Although you can, of course, use tarot cards for guided meditations at any time, they are particularly useful:

- If you are experiencing difficulty in your life with any of the 'archetypes' represented by the cards. For example, if you are struggling with the 'masculine' aspect of your self, or if there is a strong man in your life with whom you are experiencing difficulty, then the Emperor card would be a good focus for a guided meditation as this will allow you to access your authentic thoughts and feelings on the issue causing concern.
- If there is a situation in your life about which you require advice or information. For example, if you are at a cross-roads and unable to make a decision, then a guided meditation with the appropriate card could be useful. Maybe, if you are seeking to achieve justice in some matter (whether legal or otherwise), then a guided mediation centred around the Justice card could help you to access your own Wise One to

give you the counsel you need.

- If you are already working with the tarot and would like to deepen your connection with the cards and gain a clearer understanding of the imagery.

TAROT CARD GUIDED MEDITATIONS:

CARD 0: THE FOOL

In some packs The Fool is card 0 and is the first of the twenty-two Major Arcana Cards, whilst in other packs The Fool is the last of the Major cards, coming after The World.

The Fool represents the 'child' within. The part of us which 'leaps before looking'. The Fool sets out on the journey of life with simplicity and naiveté, trusting that 'all will be well'. The Fool does not prepare, does not anticipate, or organise, or approach events in a rational 'grown-up way'. The Fool rushes towards adventure, caring nothing for yesterday, not troubling to worry about the future. The 'here' and 'now' is all that matters. The message of the Fool is that sometimes we need to trust, and to take a step into the unknown.

Key words:
Reckless
Indiscreet
Naive
Foolhardy
Carefree
Spontaneous
Childlike
Frivolous
Optimistic
Trusting

CARD 1: THE MAGICIAN

The Magician represents your personal power and the way you use your skills. The Magician is skilful and adept and is able to manipulate people and circumstances according to his will. The Magician is confident, purposeful and flexible—relying on his own knowledge and abilities. The Magician makes things happen and he does this alone, without relying on others for help or guidance. He reminds us that we already know everything we need to know, and that we can achieve whatever we desire by using or developing our skills and knowledge.

Key words:
Confident
Bold
Talented
Skilful
Powerful
Manipulative
Enterprising
Adept

CARD 2: THE HIGH PRIESTESS

The High Priestess represents your intuition and psychic powers. She is both wise and intelligent and her guidance and counsel stem from a deep sense of 'inner knowing'. The High Priestess is closely associated with the Moon and with your anima or feminine aspect. She is concerned with magic and mystery and secrets and does not trouble herself with mundane matters. Instead she acts as a link between the Higher Realms and the material world. She is Priestess, sibyl, dreamer of dreams and weaver of webs—the Goddess within us all. The High Priestess reminds us to trust our intuition and the messages within our dreams, for we know far more than we think we do.

Key words:
Intuition
Femininity
Dreams
Inner Knowledge
Receptivity
Awareness

CARD 3: THE EMPRESS

The Empress also represents the anima, or feminine part of us all, but she is lush, sensual and maternal. Her drives and desires lead her to sexuality and fertility. The Empress is the eternal Earth Mother, most content and fulfilled when sustaining, and being sustained by, her family and friends. The Empress rejoices in domesticity—newly baked bread, a store cupboard of home-preserved pickles and jams, a real fire burning in the grate and flowers on the table. When her home is filled with love and laughter the Empress is truly satisfied and at ease. The Empress reminds us that these pleasures are a rich reward of this material world.

Key words:
Fertility
Maternity
Abundance
Productivity
Richness
Indulgence
Prosperity
Nurturing

CARD 4: THE EMPEROR

The Emperor represents the masculine principle, the animus within us all. He is powerful, ambitious and seeks to retain and use his authority. His domain is control, and he will aim to use his power to bring security and stability to any situation. The Emperor is aware of the benefits of financial independence and the ways in which organisation and marshalling of resources can bring rewards. Although the Emperor's main concerns are the acquisition of material possessions and the proper performance of his duties and obligations, he is at heart a benevolent figure. The Emperor tells us that the pursuit of power and material possessions can be tempered by a kind and cordial attitude.

CARD 5: THE HIEROPHANT

The Hierophant (who, in some decks is called 'The Pope'), represents your conscience; the part of you which knows that an action, even though desirable, may be unacceptable to conventional society. The Hierophant does not provide the intuitive wisdom which is the domain of the High Priestess, but rather he will offer advice and teaching regarding how best to observe the rules and systems of convention. His guiding principle is conformity and he will always seek to follow traditional guidelines. The Hierophant will always choose the straight path of morality, obedience and loyalty, never the diversion of unorthodox or unconventional thought or behaviour.

His message is that we live in a world governed by rules and regulations and we must think carefully of the consequences before we attempt to challenge them.

Key words:
Morality
Convention
Rules
Ethics
Conformity
Direction
Obedience
Tradition
Traditional Teaching

Card 6: The Lovers

The Lovers represent your ideas, ideals, hopes and feelings about relationships and love affairs. The Lovers speak of attraction, love, romance, passion, marriage, partnership. They also remind us that, quite often, in order to achieve the relationship we desire, we must make a choice. This may be the choice between two people, two situations, two ideals. United, the Lovers warn that whatever choice is finally made, it is irrevocable. There can be no half measures and no turning back. Locked in the image on the tarot card, the Lovers must remain together despite any regrets there may be. The choice has been made, for good or ill. The Lovers caution you to think deeply and choose carefully, or you may indeed get what you think you want.

Key words:
Love
Relationship
Partnership
Obsession
Infatuation
Choice
Decision
Integration
Fusion
Union

Card 7: The Chariot

The Chariot represents your self-control and self-discipline. The forces which drive the Chariot must often be channelled and controlled by the will and the intellect. Otherwise, if left to follow its own momentum, the energy of the Chariot can speed forward, out of control, leaving a trail of destruction and devastation in its wake. The Chariot speaks of harnessing your own energy and desires, and of picking a safe middle-way which will lead to safety and victory. The Chariot's message is that sometimes, in order to achieve this, it is necessary to mask your inner desires with a cloak of apparent detachment and hold firm to the Chariot's reins.

Key words:
Energy
Drive
Progress
Activity
Self-control
Determination
Victory
Triumph

CARD 8: STRENGTH

Strength (which is depicted in the Aleister Crowley pack as Lust), represents your inner strength and ability to endure despite all obstacles and setbacks. This card reminds you that no-one is ever asked to bear more than they can manage, and that you have deep reserves of courage and strength to call upon. Strength also reminds you that every problem and every difficulty is an opportunity for growth and learning. Ask yourself:

What can I learn from this? What is this teaching me?

Key words:
Courage
Endurance
Perseverance
Overcoming
Courage
Resolution
Compassion

CARD 9: THE HERMIT

The Hermit represents the part of you which requires solitude and withdrawal from the material world. The Hermit has retreated from the outer world to an inner space where peace, guidance and healing are available. There, alone, the Hermit can reflect upon the past, consider the present and contemplate the future, drawing strength from seclusion. The Hermit's message is that you need time alone. Go within to find the healing sanctuary you need. Observe, keep your counsel, live quietly and learn from the experience.

Key words:
Isolation
Retirement
Retreat
Searching
Introspection
Patience
Healing
Silence

CARD 10: THE WHEEL OF FORTUNE

The Wheel of Fortune represents the law of karma and the continuous wheel of cause and effect. This symbol reminds us that whatever we sow, we shall reap—whether fortune or misfortune, good or bad. The Wheel of Fortune also tells you that the only constant in this life is that everything must change. No matter the circumstances or the emotions, they too will pass. That everything is transient is the message of the Wheel. So whether you are experiencing the heights of happiness, joy and contentment or the depths of despair, misery and depression, the message of the Wheel is that nothing lasts. Enjoy or endure, and know that it will change.

Key words:
Karma
Cause and effect
Consequences
Change
Movement
Adapting
Transience
Cycles
Seasons

Card 11: Justice

Justice (shown in the Aleister Crowley pack as Adjustment), represents the part of you which seeks balance and equilibrium. The Justice card speaks of the desire for fairness and equity, and of the act of balancing and weighing decisions. (The Egyptian Goddess Ma'at represented essential wisdom, equilibrium and cosmic harmony. It was her task to weigh the heart of each soul who had newly passed into the Higher Realms. Each heart was weighed against an ostrich feather, which represented truth, judgement and the law, and the outcome decided the next destination of the soul.)

The message of Justice is that harmony can only be restored when a just decision has been reached, and that justice must extend to all the players in the drama of life. Consider whether you are seeking a decision or solution which is in your best interests only, or whether you are prepared to extend Justice to all concerned.

Key words:
Balance
Weighing
Equity
Fairness
Truth
Harmony
Understanding
Settlements
Verdicts
Outcomes

Card 12: The Hanged Man

The Hanged Man represents your ability to sacrifice your hopes, dreams and illusions in the certain knowledge that, in time, they will be replaced by something more valuable. The Hanged Man is suspended, upside down, in a void. He waits patiently, smiling, despite his perilous position. For he know that the suspension of action will soon revert to activity. The Hanged Man counsels you to wait, even though the void beneath your feet may seem very far below. The message of the Hanged Man is that, quite often, if you accept that sacrifice is unavoidable and you mentally prepare for it, you will not be required to follow the thought with action.

Key words:
Suspension
Stagnation
Waiting
Sacrifice
Renunciation
Surrender

CARD 13: DEATH

Death represents transformation. This may be a new perception, a new way of being or a new situation. The Death card brings liberation from the old, renewal and rebirth. Death cuts away worn-out, stagnant patterns and, having eliminated all that is no longer necessary, creates a new order.

Death's message is that the time for change may have arrived. It is part of the human condition to prefer the familiar, even if it is unsatisfactory. Embrace change, accept it and move forward to the future, leaving the past behind. In a little while your current situation will be in the past. As Kahlil Gibran says in *The Prophet*, *'Yesterday is but today's memory and tomorrow is today's dream.'*

Key words:
Transformation
Change
Severance
Renewal
Growth
Freedom
The past
The future

CARD 14: TEMPERANCE

The Temperance card (shown in the Aleister Crowley pack as Art), represents the part of you which seeks moderation and restraint. Temperance waits quietly, peacefully, for harmony to be restored. Temperance knows that, sometimes, only caution and restraint will bring about the desired outcome. The message of this card is that the gentle energy of patience, accommodation and facilitation is often far more powerful than the energy of dynamic action.

Key words:
Moderation
Consolidation
Lingering
Resting
Holding back
Patience
Calmness
Tolerance

CARD 15: THE DEVIL

The Devil represents the deeply hidden part of your subconscious which you may prefer not to recognise. The Devil is concerned with confusion and temptation and pride and obsession and all the 'negative' aspects of our selves which we prefer not to own. The Devil's message is that you have the power to break free of any limitations which are holding you back. You need not be a slave to your emotions, or to other people's whims and desires. You can break the chains of habit, or obsession or manipulation.

Key words:
Trapped
Enslaved
Frightened
Temptation
Pride
Obsession
Ignorance
Inertia

CARD 16: THE TOWER

The Tower represents your inner defences, those barriers of thought and reason which may have been acquired over a long period of time and which can be shattered, at a stroke, by external circumstances. In a tarot reading the Tower often signals sudden, unexpected change and upheaval and liberation from familiar structures, patterns and beliefs. The message of the Tower is that, in order to endure and survive, situations and relationships must be built on strong, firm foundations. Structures which crumble are fulfilling their destiny, having served their allotted time and purpose. The Tower speaks of releasing the old and preparing for the new and, above all, accepting that the Higher Realms take care that no-one is ever asked to endure more than they are capable of. The changes wrought by the Tower are unexpected and often over-whelming, but the underlying message is that liberation from old worn-out habits and structures can bring freedom and can lead to fulfilment. The Tower asks you to remember than within every unexpected difficulty there is an opportunity for growth and learning.

Key Words:
Liberation
Breakdown
Crumbling
Swiftness
Unexpected
Impermanence
Release
Upheaval
Shock
Change

CARD 17: THE STAR

The Star represents that part of you which harbours your deepest wishes, hopes and dreams. Even though your ideals and goals may be unorthodox or unconventional, perhaps even hidden away from those around you, the Star urges you to move forward to meet your destiny. The Star speaks of optimism and hope and renewal and suggests that, quite often, the way forward is along the road of Truth. The message of the Star is that you should not sacrifice your dreams and aspirations for the sake of conventionality. The Star reminds you that you have the power to create your own reality and asks you to listen to your inner Wise One, be yourself and honour your dreams.

Key words:
Hope
Wishes
Optimism
Renewal
Rejuvenation
Aspiration
Realisation
Unconventional
Inspiration
Blessings

CARD 18: THE MOON

The Moon represents your subconscious ability for self-deception. The Moon speaks of illusion and confusion and hidden feelings. Quite often we hide our feelings from ourselves, choosing not to see the reality of a situation. We do this because the reality is not what we would choose for ourselves, so we hide the truth behind a cloak of deception which fits rather more comfortably. Additionally, the Moon reminds us that we are solely responsible for our feelings. We have the power to choose between feeling angry or not angry; happy or sad. The message of the Moon is to look beneath the surface, face your subconscious fears and needs, and seek clarity and honesty beneath the surface which is presented to you.

Key words:
Illusion
Deception

Self-deception
Fluctuation
Emotion
Unreality
Fantasy
Pretence
Unknown
Undercurrents

CARD 19: THE SUN

The Sun represents your creativity. Regardless of what else
may be occurring, the Sun is a constant. A radiant beacon
of warmth and energy and clarity. We rely on the Sun to
warm the land, grow the crops and maintain the regularity
of the seasons and the message of the Sun is that, with creativity, we can overcome seemingly insurmountable obstacles. Allow your creativity to shine through to spread light
and happiness and to achieve stability and success.

Key words:
Joy
Happiness
Creativity
Light
Fruitfulness
Success
Warmth
Recognition
Appreciation
Satisfaction
Enthusiasm

CARD 20: JUDGEMENT

Judgement (named the Aeon in the Aleister Crowley pack),
represents that part of you which seeks your destiny.
Judgement reminds you that before a new pathway can be
chosen there are often difficult decisions to be faced, and
that before a new beginning there has to be an ending.
Judgement asks you to put aside your emotions and use

your discernment and discrimination to judge a situation on the basis of both past history and current events. Judgement's message is that decisions which affect the course of your life should not be taken lightly, and that assessment, reasoning and gathering and sifting the facts are of more use to you, at this point, than intuition or emotion.

Key words:
Decision
Resolution
Destiny
Understanding
Assessment
Evaluation
Ending/Beginning

CARD 21: THE WORLD

The World represents your potential; your ability to do and to achieve whatever you desire—providing you desire it sufficiently! The image, in most decks, is that of a woman dancing over the earth, and the message of this card is that we all have the inner strength and capabilities to achieve our highest potential. The World encourages you to utilise your talents, dare to develop your abilities and reach out towards your goals with courage and, if necessary, audacity. Remember, if you think you can, you undoubtedly can! So if you can, the only question which remains is—will you?

Key words:
Potential
Ability
Freedom
Visualisation
Manifestation
Attainment
Accomplishment
Realisation

- Begin by choosing the card with which you want to work. Remember, the card you choose should represent the problem about which you are seeking advice or clarification.
- Examine the image and look carefully at the shapes and the colours.

Spend at least four or five minutes fixing the image in you mind's eye.

Switch on your tape-recorder; open with chosen introduction.

You find yourself standing in a landscape... (30 seconds) Look around you, what can you see?... (30 seconds) What are the colours?... (30 seconds) What is the light like?... (15 seconds) What time of day is it?.... (15 seconds) Is it warm or cool?... (15 seconds) Look to your right and you will see a Guardian. A Being of Light who is dedicated to serve and protect you. He or she will remain with you during your time with your chosen tarot image... (30 seconds) What does your Guardian look like?... (1 minute) Is your Guardian male or female or both?... (30 seconds) What is your Guardian's name?... (1 minute) Spend a few minutes with your Guardian, taking strength from this special Being of Light who is committed to taking care of you... (2 minutes) When you are ready, follow your Guardian along the path... (10 seconds) Your Guardian is taking you to see your chosen tarot image. Look around you and take notice of where you are... (2 minutes) In the distance you see your tarot symbol, waiting for you to approach... (1 minute..) You may speak to the tarot directly or you may ask your Guardian to act as an intermediary. Which would you prefer?... (1 minute) You approach and sit or stand in front of the tarot. Your Guardian is beside you... (30 seconds) What do you want to ask the tarot?... (1 minute) What do you need to know?... (1 minute) Ask as many questions as you need, and listen carefully to everything which the tarot has to say... (3 minutes) Is there anything you would like to say to your chosen tarot image?... (2 minutes) Does your Guardian have anything to add?... (2 minutes) The tarot may wish to give you a gift. You may choose to accept this or not. You may decide that you want your Guardian to accept the gift on your behalf... (1 minute) If you have accepted a gift, now is the time to examine it... (10 seconds) What is it?... (30 seconds) What does it mean to you? What does it represent?... (2 minutes) When you are quite sure there is nothing more you want to ask or to say, thank the tarot... (1 minute) Now follow your Guardian back along the path, retracing your steps to the place where you first met your Guardian... (1 minute) Spend a few minutes more with your Guardian, as he or she may have some further information or advice for you... (3 minutes) When you are ready say good-bye, knowing that you can return to see the tarot at any time you choose... (1 minute) You are now ready to leave this inner journey... (30 seconds)

Close with your chosen departure/grounding.

CHAPTER 6 — EARTH, WATER, AIR AND FIRE

Earth my body
Water my blood
Air my breath
And fire my spirit

Native American Chant

Earth grows our food and our healing medicinal plants. Water covers 70% of the earth's surface, our bodies have a high proportion of water (40%-60% depending on body weight), and the chemistry of sea water is very similar to human blood. Without water we dehydrate rapidly and, once our body water-content reaches less than 30%, we die. Air is no less important as, when deprived of oxygen, we asphyxiate within minutes. Fire, the fourth element, warms us and enables us to retain a stable body temperature. Necessary because, once body temperature drops, hypothermia sets in and coma and death ensue. Obviously, the elements are imperative for our survival in the physical, material world.

We do, though, have an additional (albeit more subtle) connection with the elements. This connection is shown through your astrological chart which is, quite simply, a map of the heavens at the time of your birth.

Each of the astrological signs is closely connected with one of the four elements:

Astrological sign		Element
Taurus	April 21—May 20	earth
Virgo	August 22—September 22	earth
Capricorn	December 21—January 19	earth
Cancer	June 21—July 20	water
Scorpio	October 23—November 22	water
Pisces	February 19—March 20	water
Gemini	May 21—June 20	air
Libra	September 23—October 22	air
Aquarius	January 20—February 18	air
Aries	March 21— April 20	fire
Leo	July 21—August 21	fire
Sagittarius	November 23—December 20	fire

If you have had your astrological chart constructed, then you will know how many planets you have in each of the astrological signs, as well as the rising or ascendant sign at the precise moment of your birth. You may be able to see from your chart whether you have a special affinity with one or more of the elements. Perhaps most of the planets were 'sitting' in, say, fire signs at the time of your birth. Such planetary placings would give you a strong connection to fire. On the other hand, though, if none of the planets were sited in a fire sign at the time of your birth, this would show a lack of connection to that element. Alternatively, if the planets were evenly distributed, giving you a good spread across earth, water, air and fire, you would have well balanced links with each of the elements.

Even if you do not have an astrological chart to work from, your sun sign (the astrological sign which held the sun at the time of your birth), will give you one major link. You can check this by comparing your birth-date with the chart above, which shows the element connection for each of the twelve astrological signs.

Guided visualisations to connect with the four elements can help you to connect with the qualities you need, and will enable you to strengthen the links with the qualities you already possess.

THE ELEMENT OF EARTH

Earth is stabilising and grounding. Working with the element of earth will enable you to connect with the qualities of:

- practicality
- responsibility
- incarnation
- growth
- nourishment
- earth energy
- this meditation is particularly useful for anyone who has little or no earth connection in their astrological birth chart, but may be undertaken by anyone wishing to link with earth energy

EARTH ELEMENT GUIDED MEDITATION

Switch on your tape-recorder; open with chosen introduction.

You are walking in a valley... (30 seconds) All around you is lush, green vegetation... (30 seconds) Grass, trees, bushes, flowers, vines, fruit... (30 seconds) Everywhere you look you can see the gifts of the earth... (15 seconds) On either side of the valley mountains rise up to the sky... (15 seconds) The lower slopes are green and brown, green grass and rich earth... (10 seconds) Higher up you can see pink and white and grey granite, white and cream limestone... (15 seconds) And crystal clusters glinting in the sunlight. Pale green and purple, blue and gold. More gifts from the earth... (30 seconds) The ground beneath your feet is rich, dark soil... (15 seconds) Ready to give life and sustenance to the seeds blown into the valley on the wind... (15 seconds) You leave the valley floor and begin your ascent up the mountain slope... (30 seconds) All about you is the rich, heavy smell of the fertile earth and the abundant vegetation... (30 seconds) As you climb higher and higher the vegetation gives way to crystal formations, rocks and minerals... (15 seconds) And you are aware that you are in the presence of ancient and wise energies... (30 seconds) As you work your way to the summit of the slope you are aware of these energies guiding and assisting you on your journey... (1 minute) Finally you are at the peak of the mountain, looking down on the valley below... (30 seconds) You are standing on rich, dark soil fragrant with the perfume of flowers and fruit and leaves... (30 seconds) All about you are clusters of crystals vibrating with their own special energies... (1 minute) Lie on your back on the earth... (10 seconds) And feel the earth's energy pouring into your body... (1 minute) Through the palms of hands, your fingers... (1 minute) Through the soles of your feet... (1 minute) Through your back and spine and buttocks... (1 minute) Through the base of your neck and your skull... (1 minute) At every point where your body touches the earth you feel a direct connection with the earth's energy... (1 minute) And you become the earth... (30 seconds) And you become the crystals... (30 seconds) You know what the earth knows... (1 minute) And your vibrations join with the crystals and you experience their knowing too... (1 minute) Every particle of your body is flooded with vibrant energy... (1 minute) You feel empowered and deeply connected to the earth... (15 seconds) You are as one with earth energy... (5 minutes) When you are ready, thank the earth... (1 minute) And the crystals... (1 minute) And the rocks... (1 minute) Knowing that, although it time to leave the mountain, you can return whenever you choose... (10 seconds) Now begin to re-trace your steps back down the mountain... (15 seconds) Past the crystal clusters and the rocks and minerals... (30 seconds) Past the lush vegetation, the flowers, the leaves, the healing herbs... (1 minute) Until, finally, you find yourself back at the place where this inner journey began... (30 seconds)

Close with chosen departure/grounding.

THE ELEMENT OF WATER

Water is mutable, adaptable and receptive. Working with the element of water will enable you to connect with the qualities of:

- compassion
- nurturing
- intuition
- sensitivity
- receptivity
- Moon energy

This meditation is particularly useful for anyone who has little or no water connection in their astrological birth chart, but may be undertaken by anyone wishing to link with water energy

WATER ELEMENT GUIDED MEDITATION

Switch on your tape-recorder; open with chosen introduction.

You are standing at the sea shore... (30 seconds) It is a warm, moonlight night, and the full moon shines above you... (1 minute) Looking up you see a canopy of deep, dark blue sky frosted with a filigree of twinkling stars... (30 seconds) Listening, you hear the soft sound of the waves breaking on the sea shore... (1 minute) You dip your toe into the water and you are surprised at how warm it is... (15 seconds) You walk into the water, feeling the waves gently ebb and flow about your ankles... (1 minute) The surf breaking into a million tiny silver bubbles around you... (10 seconds) The water is warm and comforting... (10 seconds) Welcoming you... (15 seconds) You know that you are completely safe... (30 seconds) You walk a little further until the water is waist high and you relax into the waves... (30 seconds) The ocean gently cradles and supports you... (1 minute) You lie, weightless and suspended... (1 minute) Cradled and comforted by the warm, gentle waves... (10 seconds) A dolphin is beside you... (10 seconds) She invites you to swim with her under the moonlight... (30 seconds) Easily you swing onto her back and silver cords hold you securely so that you cannot fall... (1 minute) When you are ready, the dolphin swims out from the sea shore, across the waves... (1 minute) All about you the ocean is aware of your presence and welcomes you... (10 seconds) The waves subsiding so that your dolphin swims easily and freely through the calm, sparkling water... (10 seconds) And you are joined by other dolphins... (10 seconds) As they swim beside you, you feel their peaceful, joyful energy... (1 minute) The wind blows through your hair and, bathed in starlight and moonlight, you become a child of the sea... (1 minute) If you would like to, you may now leave your dolphin to bathe in the ocean, knowing that she will remain at your side... (10 seconds) If you wish to remain on her back you may do so... (10 seconds) You are floating, lulled and supported, comforted and caressed by the ocean... (15 seconds) You are aware only of the gentle ebb and flow of the water... (30 seconds) Supporting you, holding you safe under the moonlight... (5 minutes) When you are ready to return to the shore simply say that you wish to return and your dolphin will respond instantly... (1 minute) As you move over the waves dolphins swim around you... (30 seconds) Leaping and arcing through the air, confirming their joy at your presence... (1 minute) When you reach the shore, gently remove the silver cords which have kept you safe... (1 minute) Say farewell to your dolphin and know that she will always be here to take you on this journey to meet the ocean whenever you choose... (1 minute) You are now ready to return from this inner journey (30 seconds) Close with chosen departure/grounding.

THE ELEMENT OF AIR

Air is mercurial and quick. Working with the element of air will enable you to connect with the qualities of:
- intellect
- thought
- communication
- clarity

- consciousness
- Air energy

This meditation is particularly useful for anyone who has little or no air connection in their astrological birth chart, but may be undertaken by anyone wishing to link with air energy

AIR ELEMENT GUIDED MEDITATION

Switch on your tape-recorder; open with chosen introduction.

You are walking through a woodland glade... (30 seconds) All about you are trees and plants and flowers... (30 seconds) The breeze stirs through the glade, rustling through the leaves... (30 seconds) Blowing gently through your hair, cooling your skin... (10 seconds) You enter a clearing... (30 seconds) And there you see a blue and silver hawk waiting for you... (30 seconds) Set in his forehead is a deep blue lapis, the stone of the mind... (30 seconds) He greets you by name... (1 minute) And spreads his great silver wings in welcome and invitation... (10 seconds) You walk forward and gentle, unseen hands lift you onto his back... (15 seconds) Wrapped about with cords of blue energy you are bound to the hawk's back, completely safe, completely secure... (30 seconds) The hawk takes to the air, and you feel the wind blow around you, faster and faster... (1 minute) On the hawk's back you rise high above the earth and hover on a current of air... (1 minute) Looking down you see the earth below... (1 minute) Looking up you see blue sky and wisps of white clouds... (1 minute) The hawk rises higher, riding on the wind... (1 minute) And you experience absolute freedom... (10 seconds) The ground below rushes past... (30 seconds) You can see for miles... (30 seconds) You are carried on the wind, the hawk diving and rising, flying on the currents... (2 minutes) You become as one with the wind. Wild, fast, free and powerful... (5 minutes) Sense the power of the wind... (2 minutes) The freedom... (15 seconds) Soaring high, hovering... (1 minute) Gliding... (1 minute) Swooping back down to the earth to land safely at the point where you began... (1 minute) At a touch of your finger the blue energy cords snap, and you are standing once more on the earth... (30 seconds) The hawk bends his head towards you and you touch the deep blue lapis set into his forehead... (10 seconds) You feel the vibrations of the stone... (30 seconds) And you know that this energy is activating your intuition and your clarity of thought... (2 minutes) The hawk may have a message for you. Listen very carefully, for what he has to say is important... (2 minutes) Thank the hawk for your flight on the wind... (1 minute) And now prepare to leave this inner journey... (30 seconds)

Close with chosen departure/grounding.

THE ELEMENT OF FIRE

Fire is spirit. Working with the element of fire will enable you to connect with the qualities of:
- energy
- spirituality
- divine consciousness
- unconditional love
- Fire energy

This meditation is particularly useful for anyone who has little or no fire connection in their astrological birth chart, but may be undertaken by anyone wishing to link with fire energy

FIRE ELEMENT GUIDED MEDITATION

Switch on your tape-recorder; open with chosen introduction.

You find yourself walking on a hillside... (30 seconds) It is dusk and the sun is beginning to set on the horizon... (1 minute) The evening air is cool and fresh... (15 seconds) Close by you see a beacon and you begin to walk towards it... (1 minute) As you approach you see that the beacon is, in fact, a violet flame burning in a golden chalice... (1 minute) Walking even closer you can see that the chalice is set in the centre of a circle which is created by a ring of golden bowls set on the hillside... (1 minute) Step over the golden bowls and enter the circle... (15 seconds) As you move closer to the violet flame in the centre of the circle you experience a sense of complete inner peace and tranquillity... (1 minute) Stretch your fingers towards the flame... (10 seconds) Feel the gentle warmth pervading every part of your being... (1 minute) Look at the golden bowls and you will see, within each bowl, a single violet candle... (15 seconds) Lift the chalice containing the violet flame and begin to walk the circle... (30 seconds) Pausing beside each one of the golden bowls... (10 seconds) Touching the violet flame to the wick of the candle contained within the golden bowl... (10 seconds) Watch as the wick lights and burns with a deep golden flame which reaches high up into the night sky... (2 minutes) Continue lighting the candles. Working around the circle, lighting each candle in turn... (2 minutes) Be aware that there is violet and gold to your left... (30 seconds) Violet and gold to your right... (30 seconds) Violet and gold behind you... (30 seconds) Violet and gold in front of you... (30 seconds) You are encircled by incandescent fire, burning violet and gold against the dark night sky... (2 minutes) Stand in the centre of the circle, surrounded by fire, and hold to your heart centre the chalice containing the violet flame which burns strong and clear... (1 minute) Allow the flame to wash about you... (1 minute) Sense the unconditional love which is all around you... (30 seconds) Gaze into the violet flame and sense the flame burning away any negative thoughts or emotions which you may holding... (3 minutes) Now feel your physical body being filled with the violet flame of pure, unconditional love... (1 minute) Sense this unconditional love spreading out through your aura... (1 minute) Until you are standing in a bubble of violet flame... (30 seconds) And know that your spirit burns as brightly as this violet flame... (3 minutes) When you are ready draw the violet flame back to the chalice... (1 minute) Watch the bubble around you grow smaller and smaller... (30 seconds) Until once again you are standing in the clear night air. Replace the chalice in the centre of the circle and remain for a moment watching the candles burn with pure golden fire... (1 minute) Step out of the circle, turn and watch the circle of flame lighting up the night sky, like a beacon... (1 minute) Now make your way back to the point on the hillside where this inner journey began... (1 minute) And prepare to end the journey... (1 minute)

Close with chosen departure/grounding.

CHAPTER 7 —
WORKING WITH COLOUR

I walk in beauty
Beauty before me
Beauty behind me
And beauty all around me

Native American Chant

In 1672, Isaac Newton, the English physicist and mathe-matician, published his *New Theory about Light and Colours*, in which he described his revolutionary finding that white light is, in fact, composed of seven different colours, each of which vibrates at a different frequency.

Long before Newton, though, the importance of colour was recognised. Back in 5000 BC the Egyptians were using colour in their temples of healing. Now, in the twentieth century, psychologists have become aware of the powerful influence which colour exerts upon the human psyche. 'New' experiments with colour have been carried out which have simply reconfirmed the old knowledge. As a result, colour is being used consciously to redecorate hospitals, remand centres, prisons, factory units, offices and many other places where numbers of people live and work together. There are many colour therapists working with coloured liquids, light, crystals and oils to treat a range of physical and emotional disorders. It is now accepted that colours have the power to excite, sedate, calm and other-wise influence us physically, mentally and emotionally. Once again, the wheel has come full circle.

According to the Ancient Mystery Schools, each of the seven colours:
- red
- orange
- yellow
- green
- blue

- indigo
- violet

operates on a different vibration or ray, and has particular attributes which may be used for specific purposes. No doubt you have noticed that the list given above corresponds to the colours of the rainbow and the colours of the seven chakra system, discussed in chapter 4. Another example of Universal Order. (The only difference between the rainbow and the chakra system is that I have ascribed pink to the heart chakra, whereas some sources attribute green to this energy centre.)

Guided meditations are an excellent way to access the healing power of colour, and they may used either for yourself, or for other people. Do be sure, though, if you are working with any of these meditations for the healing of other people, that you discuss what you propose to do, and obtain the recipient's permission before you begin. This is because, as mentioned in chapter 3, by sending healing energy you are, in effect invading another person's personal space. Some people, for a whole host of reasons, do not wish to be healed. Maybe because their illness allows them to experience a level of care and attention they positively need, or perhaps they have chosen to be ill because enduring the illness is a learning process for them or their carers. So always obtain consent before you start. The only exception to this rule is if someone is unconscious or too ill to give their consent, or too young, as in the case of babies and tiny children. In these cases, listen to your inner Wise One, and do what feels right. Incidentally, animals benefits enormously from colour-work, and my cats receive colour healing on a regular basis.

1 THE RED RAY CORRESPONDENCES:

- ruby, red garnet, black obsidian
- the root chakra
- Mars
- the number one

Use the red ray if you need:
- leadership
- independence
- energy
- courage
- determination
- willpower
- spontaneity

Warning: use the red ray with great caution if you have heart or blood pressure problems. In these circumstances it would be much better to use pink instead.

RED RAY GUIDED MEDITATION

Switch on your tape-recorder; open with chosen introduction.

You find yourself on a hillside, standing in front of a small temple... (30 seconds) There is a doorway directly in front you. Open the door and step inside the temple... (1 minute) Stepping inside you find yourself in a red room... (15 seconds) The floor and walls are red... (10 seconds) The ceiling is red... (10 seconds) The light within the room is red... (10 seconds) In the centre of the room is a seat and a table. On the table you will find a red rose, a jug filled with red liquid, an empty glass and a small box.... (10 seconds) Walk to the table... (30 seconds) Open the box. Inside the box you will find a beautiful red cloak made of the lightest, finest material you can imagine... (30 seconds) Remove the cloak and slip it on... (30 seconds) As the gossamer folds of the cloak settle about you, you feel the healing energy of red... (30 seconds) Red which is filling you with strength and courage, determination and perseverance... (1 minute) Now pour the liquid into the glass and sip.... (30 seconds) And as you taste the red liquid feel the healing energy of red coursing through your veins, bringing you strength and energy, willpower and fortitude... (1 minute) Sit in the chair and take the red rose in your hand... (30 seconds) Examine the rose and look deep within the delicate curve of the petals... (1 minute) Breathe in the heady fragrance of the rose perfume... (1 minute) And feel the healing red energy stimulating, invigorating and renewing every part of your being... (5 minutes) When you are ready, remove the red cloak and, folding it carefully, return it to the box... (2 minutes) Decide now whether to return the red rose, or keep it with you... (1 minute) Take one last look around the red room... (1 minute) And then step back out onto the hillside, closing the door behind you... (30 seconds) You are now strengthened and renewed and you know that you can return to the healing power of red energy whenever you choose... (1 minute) You are now ready to return from this healing inner journey... (30 seconds)

Close with chosen departure/grounding.

2 — THE ORANGE RAY CORRESPONDENCES:

- amber, topaz
- the sacral chakra
- Sun
- the number two

Use the orange ray if you need:

- enthusiasm
- confidence
- creativity
- joy
- a sense of well-being
- health
- vitality

ORANGE RAY GUIDED MEDITATION

Switch on your tape-recorder; open with chosen introduction.

You find yourself on a hillside, standing in front of a small temple... (30 seconds) There is a doorway directly in front of you. Open the door and step inside the temple... (1 minute) Stepping inside you find yourself in a orange room... (15 seconds) The floor and walls are orange... (10 seconds) The ceiling is orange... (10 seconds) The light within the room is orange... (10 seconds) In the centre of the room is a seat and a table. On the table you will find a marigold, a jug filled with orange liquid, an empty glass and a small box.... (10 seconds) Walk to the table... (30 seconds) Open the box. Inside the box you will find a beautiful orange cloak made of the lightest, finest material you can imagine... (30 seconds) Remove the cloak and slip it on... (30 seconds) As the gossamer folds of the cloak settle about you, you feel the healing energy of orange... (30 seconds) Orange which is filling you with vitality and enthusiasm, confidence and a sense of well-being... (1 minute) Now pour the liquid into the glass and sip.... (30 seconds) And as you taste the orange liquid feel the healing energy of orange coursing through your veins, bringing you a deep sense of joy and happiness... (1 minute) Sit in the chair and take the marigold in your hand... (30 seconds) Examine the marigold and concentrate on the deep orange centre... (1 minute) Breathe in the orange energy which is flowing from the centre of the flower... (1 minute) And feel the healing orange energy bringing vitality and vigour to every part of your being... (5 minutes) When you are ready, remove the orange cloak and, folding it carefully, return it to the box... (2 minutes) Decide now whether to return the marigold, or keep it with you... (1 minute) Take one last look around the orange room... (30 seconds) And then step back out onto the hillside, closing the door behind you... (1 minute) You are now filled with vitality and joy and you know that you can return to the healing power of orange energy whenever you choose... (1 minute) You are now ready to return from this healing inner journey... (30 seconds) Close with chosen departure/grounding.

3 — THE YELLOW RAY CORRESPONDENCES:
  • yellow citrine, turquoise
  • the solar plexus chakra
  • Mercury
  • the number three

Use the yellow ray if you need:
- ideas
- knowledge and wisdom
- clarity of thought
- awareness

YELLOW RAY GUIDED MEDITATION

Switch on your tape-recorder; open with chosen introduction.

You find yourself on a hillside, standing in front of a small temple... (30 seconds) There is a doorway directly in front you. Open the door and step inside the temple... (1 minute) Stepping inside you find yourself in a yellow room... (15 seconds) The floor and walls are yellow... (10 seconds) The ceiling is yellow... (10 seconds) The light within the room is yellow... (10 seconds) In the centre of the room is a seat and a table. On the table you will find a daffodil, a jug filled with yellow liquid, an empty glass and a small box... (10 seconds) Walk to the table... (30 seconds) Open the box. Inside the box you will find a beautiful yellow cloak made of the lightest, finest material you can imagine... (30 seconds) Remove the cloak and slip it on... (30 seconds) As the gossamer folds of the cloak settle about you, you feel the healing energy of yellow... (30 seconds) Yellow which is giving you absolute clarity of thought... (1 minute) Now pour the liquid into the glass and sip... (30 seconds) And as you taste the yellow liquid feel the healing energy of yellow coursing through your veins, bringing you optimism and awareness... (1 minute) Sit in the chair and take the daffodil in your hand... (30 seconds) Examine the daffodil and look deep within the graceful sweep of the trumpet..(1 minute) Breathe in the healing power of yellow as it pours from the centre of the daffodil... (1 minute) And feel the yellow energy clearing your mind, sweeping away the cobwebs, and allowing the ideas to flow with clarity and precision... (5 minutes) When you are ready, remove the yellow cloak and, folding it carefully, return it to the box... (2 minutes) Decide now whether to return the daffodil, or keep it with you... (1

minute) Take one last look around the yellow room... (1 minute) And then step back out onto the hillside, closing the door behind you... (30 seconds) You are now filled with clarity and optimism and you know that you can return to the healing power of yellow energy whenever you choose... (1 minute) You are now ready to return from this healing inner journey..(30 seconds)
Close with chosen departure/grounding.

4 — THE GREEN RAY CORRESPONDENCES:
* rose quartz, jade
* the heart chakra
* Venus
* the number four

Use the green ray if you need:
* love
* compassion
* understanding
* balance
* harmony

GREEN RAY GUIDED MEDITATION
Switch on your tape-recorder; open with chosen introduction.

You find yourself on a hillside, standing in front of a small temple... (30 seconds) There is a doorway directly in front you. Open the door and step inside the temple... (1 minute) Stepping inside you find yourself in a green room... (15 seconds) The floor and walls are green... (10 seconds) The ceiling is green... (10 seconds) The light within the room is green... (10 seconds) In the centre of the room is a seat and a table. On the table you will find a green leaf, a jug filled with green liquid, an empty glass and a small box... (10 seconds) Walk to the table... (30 seconds) Open the box. Inside the box you will find a beautiful green cloak made of the lightest, finest material you can imagine... (15 seconds) Remove the cloak and slip it on... (30 seconds) As the gossamer folds of the cloak settle about you, you feel the healing energy of green... (30 seconds) Green which is flooding every fibre of your being with love and serenity... (1 minute) Now pour the liquid into the glass and sip... (30 seconds) And as you taste the green liquid feel the healing energy of green coursing through your veins, bringing you compassion and understanding, harmony and balance... (1 minute) Sit in the chair and take the green leaf in your hand... (30 seconds) Examine the leaf, noting the fine tracery of veins, the gentle curve of the stem... (1 minute) Breathe in the soft, green healing energy... (1 minute) And feel the healing green energy flooding every part of your being with pure, unconditional love... (5 minutes) When you are ready, remove the green cloak and, folding it carefully, return it to the box... (2 minutes) Decide now whether to return the leaf, or keep it with you... (1 minute) Take one last look around the green room... (1 minute) And then step back out onto the hillside, closing the door behind you... (30 seconds) Now radiant with the healing power of love, you know that you can return to be healed by soft green energy whenever you choose... (1 minute) You are now ready to return from this healing inner journey... (30 seconds) Close with chosen departure/grounding.

5 — THE BLUE RAY CORRESPONDENCES
- amethyst, clear quartz crystal
- the throat chakra
- Jupiter
- the number five

Use the blue ray if you need:
- faith
- trust
- serenity

BLUE RAY GUIDED MEDITATION
Switch on your tape-recorder; open with chosen introduction.
You find yourself on a hillside, standing in front of a small temple... (30 seconds) There is a doorway

directly in front you. Open the door and step inside the temple... (1 minute) Stepping inside you find yourself in a blue room... (15 seconds) The floor and walls are clear, luminous blue... (10 seconds) The ceiling is clear, luminous blue... (10 seconds) The light within the room is clear, luminous blue... (10 seconds) In the centre of the room is a seat and a table. On the table you will find a blue hyacinth, a jug filled with blue liquid, an empty glass and a small box... (10 seconds) Walk to the table... (30 seconds) Open the box. Inside the box you will find a beautiful luminous blue cloak made of the lightest, finest material you can imagine... (15 seconds) Remove the cloak and slip it on... (30 seconds) As the gossamer folds of the cloak settle about you, you feel the healing energy of blue... (30 seconds) Clear, luminous blue which is filling you with perfect serenity, perfect peace ... (1 minute) Now pour the liquid into the glass and sip... (30 seconds) And as you taste the blue liquid feel the healing energy of blue coursing through your veins, bringing you absolute trust and perfect faith that all is happening as it should, as it is intended to happen... (1 minute) Sit in the chair and take the blue hyacinth in your hand... (30 seconds) Examine each of the delicate petals which form this intricate flower... (1 minute) Breathe in the sweet perfume... (1 minute) And feel the healing blue energy calming and soothing every part of your being... (5 minutes) When you are ready, remove the blue cloak and, folding it carefully, return it to the box... (2 minutes) Decide now whether to return the hyacinth, or keep it with you... (1 minute) Take one last look around the blue room... (1 minute) And then step back out onto the hillside, closing the door behind you... (30 seconds) Now calmed and soothed, you know that you can return to the healing power of blue energy whenever you choose... (1 minute) You are now ready to return from this healing inner journey... (30 seconds)

Close with chosen departure/grounding.

6 — THE INDIGO RAY CORRESPONDENCES:

- lapis, diamond, clear quartz crystal
- the brow chakra
- Saturn
- the number six

Use the indigo ray if you need:

- acceptance
- organisation
- responsibility
- ability to use power wisely

INDIGO RAY GUIDED MEDITATION

Switch on your tape-recorder; open with chosen introduction.

You find yourself on a hillside, standing in front of a small temple... (30 seconds) There is a doorway directly in front you. Open the door and step inside the temple... (1 minute) Stepping inside you find yourself in an indigo room... (15 seconds) The floor and walls are deep indigo blue... (15 seconds) The ceiling is deep indigo blue... (10 seconds) The light within the room is deep indigo blue... (10 seconds) In the centre of the room is a seat and a table. On the table you will find a deep indigo blue carnation, a jug filled with indigo liquid, an empty glass and a small box... (10 seconds) Walk to the table... (30 seconds) Open the box. Inside the box you will find a beautiful deep indigo blue cloak made of the lightest, finest material you can imagine... (15 seconds) Remove the cloak and slip it on... (30 seconds) As the gossamer folds of the cloak settle about you, you feel the healing energy of indigo ... (30 seconds) Deep indigo blue which is giving you a complete understanding of the nature of power and responsibility... (1 minute) Now pour the liquid into the glass and sip... (30 seconds) And as you taste the indigo liquid feel the healing energy of deep indigo blue coursing through your veins, bringing you a sense of unity and acceptance... (1 minute) Sit in the chair and take the carnation in your hand... (30 seconds) Examine the delicate and intricate pattern of the petals... (1 minute) Breathe in the heady fragrance of the carnation perfume... (1 minute) And feel the healing deep indigo blue energy focusing and stabilising every part of your being... (5 minutes) When you are ready, remove the indigo cloak and, folding it carefully, return it to the box... (2 minutes) Decide now whether to return the carnation, or keep it with you... (1 minute) Take one last look around the indigo room... (1 minute) And then step back out onto the hillside, closing the door behind you... (30 seconds) You are now focused and centred and you know that you can return to the healing power of indigo blue energy whenever you choose... (1 minute) You are now ready to return from this healing inner journey... (30 seconds)

Close with chosen departure/grounding.

7 — THE VIOLET RAY CORRESPONDENCES:
- amethyst, clear quartz crystal
- the crown chakra
- Moon
- the number seven

Use the violet ray if you need:
- inspiration
- intuition
- spirituality

VIOLET RAY GUIDED MEDITATION

Switch on your tape-recorder; open with chosen introduction.

You find yourself on a hillside, standing in front of a small temple... (30 seconds) There is a doorway directly in front you. Open the door and step inside the temple... (1 minute) Stepping inside you find yourself in a violet room... (15 seconds) The floor and walls are violet... (10 seconds) The ceiling is violet... (10 seconds) The light within the room is violet... (10 seconds) In the centre of the room is a seat and a table. On the table you will find a spray of lilac, a jug filled with violet liquid, an empty glass and a small box... (10 seconds) Walk to the table... (30 seconds) Open the box. Inside the box you will find a beautiful violet cloak made of the lightest, finest material you can imagine... (15 seconds) Remove the cloak and slip it on... (30 seconds) As the gossamer folds of the cloak settle about you, you feel the healing energy of violet... (30 seconds) Violet which is expanding your intuition and making you aware of the connections between every living thing... (2 minutes) Now pour the liquid into the glass and sip... (30 seconds) And as you taste the violet liquid feel the healing energy of violet coursing through your veins, bringing you an awareness of your connection with the Source... (2 minutes) Sit in the chair and take the spray of lilac in your hand... (30 seconds) Examine the spray and look deep within the heart of each individual flower... (1 minute) Breathe in the heady fragrance of the lilac perfume... (1 minute) And feel the healing violet energy creating a bridge between your physical, earthly body and your Higher Self... (7 minutes) When you are ready, remove the violet cloak and, folding it carefully, return it to the box... (2 minutes) Decide now whether to return the lilac spray, or keep it with you... (1 minute) Take one last look around the violet room... (1 minute) And then step back out onto the hillside, closing the door behind you... (30 seconds) You are now inspired and infused with a sense of perfect peace, knowing that you can return to the healing power of violet energy whenever you choose... (1 minute) You are now ready to return from this healing inner journey... (1 minute)

Close with chosen departure/grounding.

CHAPTER 8 — WOMEN'S MYSTERIES

We are the flow and we are the ebb
We are the weaver, we are the web

Native American Chant

Although William Shakespeare spoke of the 'seven ages of man', I believe that women have their own, very special and specific 'ages' and cycles.

These are:

AGE 1 HOUR TO 12 YEARS:

Keywords: innocence, virginity

During this cycle of women's lives we should experience total acceptance of ourselves as unique and fragile individuals. During this precious time, our innocence and vulnerability should be both celebrated and protected.

AGE 12 YEARS—32 YEARS:

Keywords: fertility, abundance

With the onset of puberty and the menstrual cycle we should be able to celebrate our femininity through sexual love and motherhood (if we choose to), and through the forging of deep and enduring relationships with loving partners.

AGE 32 YEARS TO 55 YEARS:

Keywords: expression, direction

During this time we should be able to continue the theme of relationships, but also advance into the world about us, expanding and exploring, acquiring additional knowledge and skills and contributing our own, individual talents and abilities.

AGE 55 YEARS ONWARDS:

Keywords: wisdom, connection

By now we should be comfortable with ourselves, our bodies and our connection with both the down-to-earth, concrete, practicalities of daily living and the spiritual dimension of this, our chosen incarnation. We should know 'why we are here' and 'what we should be doing' and we should be able to guide and heal others through our wisdom, understanding and personal power.

Unfortunately, life being what it is, this pattern rarely emerges. Instead of innocence and virginity being nurtured and safeguarded, many women are subjected to rejection and physical, sexual, mental and emotional abuse from an early age. We learn to grow up very quickly and acquire the first layers of self-defence and a mask or two to protect us from further pain.

As we mature, although some of us are lucky enough to create deeply loving relationships, for many women the story unfolds quite differently.

Relationships may be painful, difficult, unrewarding, even violent. Pregnancies may be terminated, or unwanted. Some women may, happily and hopefully, bring healthy, beautiful children into the world, only to find they do not have the resources available to care for them as they would like. Life becomes an exhausting struggle and so women, in self-defence, create further layers and another mask to defend that fragile inner core.

Far from having an opportunity to expand and develop, many women find that their middle years are a time of personal sacrifice, undertaken to enable the family to flourish.

And finally, for many women, the arrival of the menopause is not a confirmation of their wisdom and maturity, but rather a signal that their cycle of usefulness and productivity has come to an end. This can be the most painful, the most traumatic time in a woman's life. When she, mistakenly, perceives herself as no longer either fruitful, desirable or useful.

Guided meditations can help you to reconnect with your

past and help you to heal the wounds inflicted upon you
during each of the cycles described. They can also be used
to reunite you with your femininity and enable you to reaf-
firm your delight in womanhood.

GUIDED MEDITATION
AGE 1 HOUR—12 YEARS

Keywords: innocence and virginity
- Work with this meditation if you want to heal the
  wounds you have acquired during this first, most vulnerable, cycle of your life.

Switch on your tape-recorder; open with chosen introduction.
You find yourself walking along a corridor. The walls
of the corridor are pale, translucent marble. The
floor on which you walk is slightly warm and yielding.
Walking is effortless... (1 minute) As you walk you pass
crystals of all shapes and colours and sizes. You are aware
of their gentle healing energy, washing over you... (1
minute) Ahead, you see a marble pool. An oasis of water
surrounded by candles. The flickering flames cast a gentle, welcoming glow... (30 seconds) The air is cool and
fragrant... (30 seconds) As you approach the pool a
woman steps forward, smiling in welcome. She is the
Moon Goddess, dressed in white. Around her neck
hangs a crystal of incredible purity and power. She ges-
tures you forward... (30 seconds) Gently, tenderly, with
care and sensitivity, she helps you to undress... (1
minute) She leads you by the hand to the pool of clear,
fragrant water... (1 minute) Slide into the water and
float... (15 seconds) You float, suspended in the water,
gently held in the warm fragrance, bathed in gentle,
healing, eternal energy... (3 minutes) Here, in this
sacred, healing temple, speak to the Moon Goddess of
the pain you have experienced. Take your time to tell
your story, knowing that there will be no questions, no
criticism, no condemnation, no judgement... (5 minutes)
As your story unfolds feel the healing energy of the fra-

grant water, and the healing love of the Moon Goddess... (3 minutes) When you have finished your story, allow the Moon Goddess to help you from the pool, dry your body... (2 minutes) Enfold you in a cloak of purest white. A cloak which drapes about you, from head to toe, absorbing all the negative energy which you have accumulated since you were born... (1 minute) Allow the Moon Goddess to hold you gently so that you may feel the power of her unconditional love begin to heal the wounds... (5 minutes) Know that she will always be here for you. To listen to your story. To bring you healing energy. To remind you of the power she wields for all wounded women... (2 minutes) Return the cloak... (1 minute) Retrace your steps back along the corridor... (2 minutes) To the place where this healing inner journey began... (1 minute)

Close with chosen departure/grounding.

GUIDED MEDITATION
AGE 12 YEARS—32 YEARS

Keywords: fertility and abundance

• Work with this meditation if you want to heal the wounds acquired during this second cycle of your life

Switch on your tape-recorder; open with chosen introduction.

You are walking in an orchard... (30 seconds) All about you is the abundance of the earth... (30 seconds) Apple and pear trees, oranges and lemons, grapes and nectarines flourish in a tangle of fertile growth... (30 seconds) There are flowers growing everywhere... (30 seconds) The orchard is alive with colour and fragrance and life... (1 minute) As you walk you are joined by two women. The Moon Goddess to your left, draped in silver cloth and the pale light of the Moon. To your right, the Sun Goddess, wearing cloth of gold, with Sunlight in her hair. They take your hands and walk serenely beside you... (2 minutes) You take strength and courage from their presence... (2 minutes) At last, you find yourself in

a small clearing... (30 seconds) Birds fly overhead and looking up, through the branches of the trees, you see both the Sun and the Moon... (30 seconds) You sit on the grass, Moon Goddess to your left, Sun Goddess to your right, and you speak of everything which you have had to do in order to survive. Knowing there will no questions, no criticism, no condemnation, no judgement... (5 minutes) Feel the healing presence and unconditional love of the two Goddesses beside you... (2 minutes) When your truth has been told, allow the Moon Goddess to help you to your feet... (1 minute) Watch as she draws down the silver healing rays of the Moon to cleanse and clear every part of your being, at every level... (1 minute) Feel the cool healing rays of the Moonlight wash over you, beginning to heal the wounds... (2 minutes) Now the Sun Goddess is at your side, and she is drawing down the golden healing rays of the Sun to revitalise and rejuvenate every part of your being, at every level... (1 minute) Feel the warm healing rays of the Sunlight wash over you, helping to heal the wounds... (2 minutes) Now form a circle with the Moon Goddess to your left, and the Sun Goddess to your right, and allow their gentle energy and unconditional love to flood through your senses, cleansing, clearing and healing... (5 minutes) Know that the Moon Goddess and the Sun Goddess will always be here for you to channel the cleansing, healing powers of the Moon and Sun. To remind you of the strength they can give to all wounded women... (1 minute) Now begin to re-trace your steps back through the orchard... (1 minute) And prepare to leave this healing inner journey... (1 minute)
Close with chosen departure/grounding.

GUIDED MEDITATION
AGE 32 YEARS—55 YEARS
Keywords: expression and direction
- Work with this meditation if you want to heal the wounds acquired during the third cycle of your life

Switch on your tape-recorder; open with chosen introduction.

You find yourself on a hillside... (30 seconds) Ahead of you is a narrow, winding path... (30 seconds) Walk the path to the top of the hill... (1 minute) Standing on the hilltop, you can see your destination, the Crystal City, in the valley below... (1 minute) Make your way down the hillside... (1 minute) Towards the shimmering, sparkling Crystal City... (30 seconds) As you approach you can see that the city walls are made of pure crystal, sparkling and shimmering, reflecting sunlight in all directions... (2 minutes) As you approach a Guardian asks you to give your name... (30 seconds) As you speak your name a portion of the city wall slides open and you enter... (30 seconds) Within the walls are cool fountains and shaded courtyards... (1 minute) Delicate flowers... (30 seconds) And brightly coloured birds... (30 seconds) You follow the central path to a crystal globe, which is your destination... (1 minute) As you approach Guardians greet you by name, smiling their welcome... (1 minute) You enter the crystal globe... (30 seconds) Seated in the centre of the crystal globe, beside a silver chest, is the Moon Goddess... (30 seconds) Walk towards her... (30 seconds) She smiles and opens her arms in greeting... (15 seconds) You sit beside her, rest against her shoulder and begin to tell your story. Speak to the Moon Goddess of your pain, your disappointment, your frustration, your rage. You may open your heart to her, knowing there will be no questions, no criticism, no condemnation, no judgement... (5 minutes) When you have said all there is to say, watch as the Moon Goddess walks to a silver chest... (1 minute) She removes a silver sword. The handle is ornate and set with many crystals. The gleaming blade bears your name, etched into the metal. She hands you the sword and you know that this is the sword of courage, sharp enough and strong to cut the negative ties with the past... (30 seconds) Hold the sword. Feel its strength and power... (3 minutes) The Moon Goddess now takes from the chest a silver shield. This, too, is set with many crystals and is etched with your name... (15 seconds) Take the shield, knowing that this is the shield of protection... (15 seconds) Hold the shield. Feels its strength and power... (3 minutes) Know that you can call upon the warrior strength of the sword of courage, and the protective energy of the shield of protection whenever you choose. They bear your name, they have been gifted to you by the Moon Goddess... (2 minutes) Return these gifts to the Moon Goddess, knowing that they are available to you whenever you need them. Know that the Moon Goddess will always be here for you. To listen to your story. To bring you healing energy. To remind you of the strength and courage she can give to all vulnerable women... (2 minutes) Now prepare to leave the crystal globe... (1 minute) Outside in the sunlight, retrace your steps through the Crystal City... (1 minute) Past the courtyards and fountains... (30 seconds) Past the Guardian at the gate who waves farewell... (30 seconds). Out onto the hillside... (15 seconds) Across the valley... (30 seconds) Up to the top of the hill... (30 seconds) Down the narrow, winding path... (15 seconds) Back to the place where this healing inner journey began... (30 seconds)

Close with chosen departure/grounding.

GUIDED MEDITATION
AGE 55 YEARS ONWARDS

Keywords: wisdom and connection
 • Work with this meditation if you want to heal the wounds acquired during the fourth and final cycle.

Switch on your tape-recorder; open with chosen introduction.

You find yourself standing beside the ocean... (30 seconds) The moon is reflected on the water, silver on midnight blue... (30 seconds) Listen to the sound of the ocean, calling to you... (1 minute) Look up to the night sky and see the stars, shining silver against the deep velvet blue ... (1 minute) The moon, casting her gentle light all about you... (30 seconds) Turn to your right, and you will see the Moon Goddess, wreathed in a cloak of silver and lit by starlight... (30 seconds) She smiles in welcome and holds her hands out to you. Walk towards her ... (30 seconds) Around her neck hangs a crystal of incredible purity and power. When you are standing beside her she removes the crystal and places it about your neck... (2 minutes) The crystal, hanging from its silver chain, lies directly at your heart centre and you feel its gentle, healing power wash over you... (3 minutes) The Moon Goddess takes your hand and you walk with her, bathed in moonlight and starlight, and speak to her of your life. You may tell her everything. Speak of your successes and your failures, your desires and your regrets. You may do this, knowing there will be no questions, no criticism, no condemnation, no judgement... (5 minutes) When you have said everything you need to say the Moon Goddess takes from beneath her cloak a book... (30 seconds) It is a silver book and on the cover your name is etched into the metal... (15 seconds) This book contains all the wisdom of women. All the wisdom you already hold. The book is merely a reminder to you of what you already know... (30 seconds) Under the moonlight, holding your book of wisdom, wearing the crystal of knowledge, take from the Moon Goddess the power which she gladly gives to you... (1 minute) Regain your inner knowledge and feel the power of womanhood... (30 seconds) Feel the energy surge through your body, mind and spirit, renewing every level of your being... (3 minutes) When you are ready, return your book and the crystal to the Moon Goddess. Knowing that she will safeguard these for you until you need them again... (1 minute) Say farewell and, turning, begin to retrace your steps... (1 minute) Under them moonlight... (30 seconds) Listening to the ocean... (30 seconds) Until you find yourself back at the place where this healing inner journey began... (30 seconds)

Close with chosen departure/grounding.

CHAPTER 9 —
WHAT DO YOU WANT?

*Getting clear about what you
want is the first step in
materialising your goals.*

Stuart Wilde*

Not having goals in life is rather like setting out on a long
journey without having a destination. If you don't know
where you are going, you can't know how you will get there
or how long it will take, and you certainly will not know
when you have arrived! Instead, you will drift like a
motorist lost in the fog, going round and round in circles,
wanting to arrive, but not knowing the name or location of
your destination.

Of course many people live their lives without setting
goals. Goals represent desires such as a house in the country or £100,000 in the bank or travel or to be of service to
other people. Of course, many people simply cannot set
goals because they don't know what they really want. They
just accept whatever it is they have, and live from day to
day, accompanied by a deep sense of frustration and long-
ing. Hoping for something better to materialise, but not
having a clear idea of what would be better.

Only you know what you really want. Not what you
'ought' to want, or what other people think you want, or
what someone in your circumstances, at your age, should
'settle for'. The real key to having what you want is finding
out, from your inner Wise One what it is, at the inner core
of your being, you really desire. What it is that will make
you really happy, fulfilled and contented. Then, once you
are connected to your real, inner needs, you can begin to
bring them into reality.

The guided meditations which follow will enable you to

Affirmations/Stuart Wilde: White Dove International (1987) find out, from yourself, exactly and precisely, what is you really and truly want.

You may be surprised. You may be shocked. You may be delighted.

After working with the meditations, you may decide to do nothing. To allow life to continue to follow its regular course. On the other hand, though, when you find out what you really want, you may decide to turn your world upside down in order to be authentic. Be warned, this is powerful medicine, and should not be undertaken lightly !

WHAT DO YOU WANT?
MEDITATION NO. 1

- To access your thoughts and feelings on what you want with regard to family, friends, work and home.

Switch on your tape-recorder; open with chosen introduction.

You find yourself walking in a meadow... (30 seconds) It is a warm and sunny day. Looking around you see flowers and birds... (30 seconds) Continue walking until you come to a carpet which is laid on the grass, waiting for you... (1 minute) This is a magic carpet which special powers which will enable you to see clearly... (30 seconds) What colour is the carpet?... (30 seconds) Does it have a pattern? What is the pattern like?... (30 seconds) Step onto the carpet and you will find there are cords or ties which you can use to strap yourself on, so that you cannot fall off... (1 minute) Fasten the ties, making sure that you feel completely secure, completely comfortable... (1 minute) Now that you are settled simply touch the carpet with your right hand... (10 seconds) And you will find that it gently takes to the air and hovers over the meadow... (30 seconds) What does the meadow look like from this vantage point?... (30 seconds) Has anything changed?... (30 seconds) The carpet moves a little higher and, looking down, you see some people beginning to appear in the meadow below... (30 seconds) These people are your family... (30 seconds) Observe them as they

gather in the meadow... (1 minute) What are your feelings towards them?... (2 minutes) Now see your work arriving in the meadow... (1 minute) How do you feel about your work? What does it mean to you?... (2 minutes) Your home has arrived now. How do you feel about your home?... (2 minutes) Your family is now being joined by your closest friends, your acquaintances and your work colleagues... (1 minute) How do you feel about these people?... (2 minutes) Now imagine that you have a magic wand in your right hand. To make the magic work, all you have to do is point the wand... (10 seconds) Point the magic wand at your family and see them as you would really like them to be... (1 minute) In what way have they changed?... (1 minute) Now point your magic wand at your closest friends and your acquaintances... (10 seconds) In what way have they changed?... (1 minute) Now focus on your work and point your magic wand so that your work changes into what you would really like it to be... (1 minute) How has your work changed?... (2 minutes) Now pay attention to your work colleagues and point your magic wand... (1 minute) In what way are they different?... (1 minute) Now point your magic wand at your home and see it change into the home you would really like... (2 minutes) How has it changed? What is different?... (2 minutes) Looking down from the safety of your magic carpet, spread below you is your life, your world, as you would really like it to be... (10 seconds) Take notice of everything which has changed. These changes are the changes you really want .... (3 minutes) Now it is time for family, friends, work and home to leave the meadow. Wave your magic wand and they will disappear... (30 seconds) Touch your right hand to the magic carpet and it will begin a slow and gentle descent back down to the meadow.... (1 minute) Land lightly and safely... (30 seconds) Untie the cords which have held you... (15 seconds) Step onto the grass and retrace your steps across the meadow to where this inner journey began... (1 minute)
Close with chosen departure/grounding.

What do you want?
Meditation no. 2

- To access your thoughts and feelings on what you want with regard to loving relationships.

Switch on your tape-recorder; open with chosen introduction.

You are walking beside a lake... (30 seconds) The water is as still and clear as glass... (30 seconds) At the edge of the lake you will a brightly painted boat which is moored there... (10 seconds) Walk towards the boat and step inside... (1 minute) Allow the boat to drift out to the centre of the lake to where another similar, but empty, boat is waiting for you... (1 minute) On the deck of your own boat you will find a magic wand. To make the magic work, all you have to do is point the wand... (30 seconds) Point your magic wand at the other boat. Appearing in the other boat is the person you really want to share your life with... (2 minutes) Do you know this person?... (10 seconds) Is it your current life partner?... (10 seconds) If it is, has he or she changed in any way?... (10 seconds) In what way has he or she changed?... (30 seconds) Is the person in the other boat the gender you expected?... (30 seconds) Is the person in the other boat the age you expected?... (30 seconds) What are you learning from this?... (3 minutes) Do you want to ask anything of the person in the other boat? What do you want to know?... (3 minutes) Do they reply? What do they say?..... (3 minutes) Perhaps there isn't anyone in the other boat .... (10 seconds) What are you learning from this?... (3 minutes) Have you learned everything you need to know?... (3 minutes). Now allow your boat to return to the lake shore... (1 minute) Moor the boat .... (1 minute) And begin to retrace your steps to the place where you began this inner journey... (1 minute)

Close with chosen departure/grounding.

WHAT DO YOU WANT?
MEDITATION NO.3

- To access your thoughts and feelings on what you want with regard to prosperity.

Switch on your tape-recorder; open with chosen introduction.

You find yourself standing outside a giant cupboard. The cupboard is much, much taller than you are, and much, much wider... (1 minute) What colour is the cupboard?... (30 seconds) What is the cupboard made of?.... (30 seconds) There are handles on the cupboard doors. What do the handles look like?... (30 seconds) With both hands firmly grasp the cupboard door handles and pull the doors wide open... (30 seconds) Inside the cupboard you will see the amount of prosperity you really want... What can you see? Are there bank notes? Coins? Jewels? Title Deeds to properties? What kinds of properties?... (3 minutes) What else is in the cupboard?... (3 minutes) Are there any surprising or astonishing things in the cupboard?... (3 minutes) How full or empty is the cupboard?... (1 minute) Did you expect to find more or less in the cupboard?... (1 minute) What do the contents of the cupboard tell you about your attitude to prosperity?... (3 minutes) When you are ready, carefully close the cupboard doors, making sure they are tightly shut... (2 minutes) Now prepare to leave this inner journey... (1 minute)

Close with chosen departure/grounding.

WHAT DO YOU WANT?
MEDITATION NO.4

- To access your thoughts and feelings on what you want with regard to your health.

Switch on your tape-recorder; open with chosen introduction.

You find yourself in a forest glade... (30 seconds) You walk beside tall trees.... (30 seconds) Past clumps of wild flowers... (30 seconds) And small streams... (30 seconds) Ahead of you, you can see a large mirror set amongst the trees and flowers... This is a magic mirror which both shows you how you are now and how you really want to be... (30 seconds) Walk to the magic mirror and gaze at your reflection. You will see yourself as you are at the moment... (2 minutes) How do you look?... (1 minute) Do you look well?... (1 minute) If you have any illnesses you are aware of, these will be reflected in the mirror... (30 seconds) Now watch your image dissolve and see a new image form... (2 minutes) This is how you really want to be... (30 seconds) How do you look?... (30 seconds) Do you look well?... (2 minutes) Has your ill health disappeared, or is it still with you?... (1 minute) If it is still with you, why do you think that is?... (3 minutes) What purpose does your ill health serve? What use is it to you?... (3 minutes) Why do you wish to retain it?... (2 minutes) What are you learning from this?... (3 minutes) When you are ready, allow the image in the mirror to dissolve... (2 minutes) You have learned everything you need to know... (10 seconds) Now retrace your steps, back to the place in the forest glade where this inner journey began... (1 minute)

Close with chosen departure/grounding.

WHAT DO YOU WANT? MEDITATION NO.5

- To access your thoughts and feelings on what you want with regard to fulfilling the purpose of this incarnation.

Switch on your tape-recorder; open with chosen introduction.

You find yourself outside a building. It is a very large and old building. Leading up to the heavy oak doors, there are five steps... (5 seconds) You climb the steps... (5 seconds) One... (10 seconds) Two... (10 seconds) Three... (10 seconds) Four... (10 seconds) Five... (10 seconds) And now you push against the heavy oak doors which swing open to allow you to enter... (15 seconds) Step inside and you find yourself inside an enormous, high-ceilinged room. The walls are lined with shelves, and the shelves are filled with books of all kinds. Walk along the shelves and look for the book which bears your name on the spine... (2 minutes) You will need to look carefully, but it is here... (1 minute) When you find your book remove it from the shelf and carry it a nearby reading table. Lay the book down. What kind of book is it? What colour is it? Is it very old? Or is it new?... (2 minutes) Now examine the cover. What does it say?... (1 minute) In a moment you are going to open your book and you will read about yourself. You will discover the purpose of this, your present incarnation, and you will read what it is you are supposed to learn this time... (1 minute) When you are ready, open the book and begin to read... (5 minutes) When you have finished reading, return the book to the shelf where you found it... (2 minutes) Turning, you will see that the librarian is waiting to speak with you. The librarian will answer any questions you may have... (10 seconds) What do you want to know? Ask your questions now... (3 minutes) Listen very carefully to everything the librarian has to say... (5 minutes) When you are satisfied that you have obtained all the information you need to help you to fulfil the purpose of this incarnation, leave the library, closing the heavy doors behind you... (2 minutes) Walk down the steps... (5 seconds) Five... (15 seconds) Four... (15 seconds) Three... (15 seconds) Two... (15 seconds) One... (15 seconds) And find yourself back at the place where this inner journey began... (1 minute)

Close with chosen departure/grounding.

CHAPTER 10 — CREATING YOUR OWN REALITY

Hold ever before you the thought of prosperity and abundance, and know that doing so sets into operation forces that will bring it into being. The more positive you are, the quicker it will come about.

Eileen Caddy [*]

If you can think it, you can have it! Thought is the most powerful creative energy we have here in the material world. Look about you. Everything in your home, work environment, neighbourhood has been created by the power of thought. "Nonsense!" you may be thinking. "I bought this book I'm reading in the book shop, and the chair I'm sitting on is really 'real'. No-one 'thought' them for me. The telephone is supplied by the phone company and I don't 'think' paying the bill, I really do pay it..." and so on.

But wait a moment. Everything is created by the power of thought. I had to have the idea of writing this book, and then think about it, and then put the thoughts on paper. Through the process of writing I brought the thoughts into concrete reality. So did the person who designed the chair you are sitting on, the home you live in, the bed you sleep on, the fire which heats your room, the cup you drink from, the phone you use, the television you watch ... and so on. Even your garden or allotment is the product of your thoughts, because you have had to choose the plants and seeds, create the 'pattern' or design of the garden, fertilise, prune, shelter and nurture the growth. Untended, and left to its own devices, your garden or plot of land would quick-

[*]*Opening Doors Within*/Eileen Caddy, Findhorn Press (1986)

ly run riot. Weeds and pests would take over and your concept of how it should be would be dramatically changed. You retain the shape and form and concept of your garden (and everything else in your life), through the power of thought.

The thought comes first, and everything flows from that. This basic truth is now being recognised by psychologists throughout the world, and guided meditations form a central part of most sports training at international level. Sportsmen and women are trained to think of their ideal performance. They use guided meditation techniques to imagine (form an image of in the mind), not only the ideal performance, but also the energy, power and joy of winning. This technique has helped many professional athletes, skaters, golfers, swimmers and so on, not only to win, but to break world records and exceed their own 'personal best' performances.

Many, many people, including Shakti Gawain, Stuart Wilde and Eileen Caddy have written about 'Prosperity Consciousness'. The ability to create prosperity and abundance in every part of your life - money, health, love and relationships - through the power of thought.

It is as though, once we know what we really want, and we imagine it coming into reality, the Universe will supply it.

"Ah," you may say, "I've tried that, and it doesn't work! I've thought and thought and yearned with all my being, and I still didn't get what I wanted!"

There are three factors which must be present if you are to manifest your requirements. The first factor is being absolutely clear about what you want. If you decide you want a Loving Relationship, you will get it. But it may not be the kind of loving relationship you hoped for. Perhaps the loving relationship which manifests will be with a close friend on a purely platonic level. Loving? Yes! What you thought you would get? Absolutely not! The reason for this apparent mismatch is that before creating the ideal loving relationship, you must know precisely and exactly the kind of relationship you desire, and be ready to accept it completely, warts and all!

This brings us on the second factor which is necessary for success. You must be ready to accept your new reality. In my view this is perhaps the real key to success in the process of personal creativity. Time and time and time again, in my own life, I have worked on creating a new reality which has not materialised at the time I wanted it. Later, looking back, I have realised that the new reality could not materialise because I was not ready to accept it at that time. Oddly enough, though, in almost every instance the reality I worked at creating has arrived at a much later date. By then, though, even though I may have been ready, my wants may have shifted, and I have viewed my newly arrived 'creation' from an altogether different perspective - I wanted this then, but I don't want it now! I have noticed, though, that even though the 'wanting' at a conscious level may have dissipated, I have always be ready to deal with the manifestation, both at the mundane, practical level, and at the emotional and spiritual levels too.

I believe this paradox arises because our own Inner Wise One knows, absolutely, what is right for us. Although we may believe, at an outer, conscious level that we really, really want something, our Wise One knows that we are neither physically, emotionally nor spiritually prepared to deal with the new experiences. So, our Wise One guides us to make decisions or take actions which will, in fact, prevent us from having what we think we want. This is the 'Shooting Yourself In The Foot' Syndrome. Have you ever missed a really important appointment because you uncharacteristically overslept? Have you ever destroyed a blossoming relationship with seemingly irrational behaviour? Have you ever, on the spur-of-the-moment, spent money which you had ear-marked for a special and important purpose? These are all the hallmarks of 'Shooting Yourself in the Foot', and show that your Wise One is working hard on your behalf. Trust your Wise One to know what is best for you, at all levels.

When you create an inner dialogue, life becomes much simpler and much easier. By all means still want things to happen in your life, but take notice of what I call the 'inner signs and signals'. If I decide I want something to change in my life and it 'feels comfortable', then I know my Wise One approves. If, on the other hand, whenever I think of the change I desire there is any hint of physical discomfort or unease, or worry or concern or nagging doubt, then I recognise the signal. I may still want the change, but I accept, at a deep level, that it is not in my best interests, and I begin to think about other changes I might want as well. So, although I don't abandon the idea, I do 'put it at the back of my mind' and get on with life.

Assuming that you get approval from your Wise One, there is a great to do to ensure that, when your reality arrives, you are capable of dealing with it.

If, for example, you are currently employed, but really want to run your own business, don't imagine that a ready-made company will drop out of the sky. You are probably not ready for it! Plan ahead and work on acquiring the skills you will need. For example, you may need to learn about computers and book-keeping. You may need to delve into employment law and brush-up your language skills. You may have to return to part-time education in order to acquire a qualification or update your existing knowledge. You may find it necessary to re-arrange your living space, or move house, or look for premises in order to accommodate the business. You may have to work out new parameters for relationships with family and partner. And so on. When all the ground-work has been done you will be ready to run a business, and the opportunity to do so will arise. If you still want this new reality (and bear in mind, after all the preparation has been done and you have had a 'taster' of what it would really be like, you may decide that this is not the path you wish to travel), then grab the opportunity with both hands.

If you, for instance, live in a busy urban area and your idea of bliss is a reclusive country life, your new reality will not arrive unless you can handle it. Say, for example, that living in the country would mean losing contact with your family and friends, giving up your spare-time interests because of the distance involved, having no way of earning a living because of the travelling costs such a move would generate, risking the breakdown of a viable and important partnership, then your country cottage will not materialise unless these sacrifices are in your best interests. However, when all these factors have been taken into account and dealt with, one way or another, you will be ready to move into your new reality.

The third and final factor is confidence. Be assured that anxiety and doubt will prevent you from manifesting what you want. If you spend time creating your reality and then spend time thinking, "It won't work," "It can't happen," "Will it happen?" "I don't deserve it to happen," and so on, the negative energy created by the worry will effectively erase the positive energy you have generated through your guided meditation.

So, decide what you want, consult your Wise One, obtain approval, prepare thoroughly and then relax. Get on with your life. Do not wait to see what will happen, simply watch what happens. You can be sure that amazing things will happen.

CREATING YOUR OWN REALITY GUIDED MEDITATION

Switch on your tape-recorder; open with chosen introduction. You find yourself walking along a country road... (30 seconds) It is night-time and the sky above is a deep blue canopy, scattered with a sprinkling of brilliant stars... (30 seconds) Trees, their branches gently bending in the gentle breeze, reach up to the night sky... (30 seconds) The soft radiance of the moon lights your way... (30 seconds) Ahead, on the path, you see a small building... (30 seconds) Approach and you will see there is a door... (30 seconds) Push the door open and step inside, gently closing the door behind you... (15 seconds) Once inside the temple look around you. This is your inner sanctuary. Your very own, very special, private place. No-one else may enter here... (30 seconds) Because this is your sanctuary it is designed to suit your needs... (10 seconds) Look around you. What are the colours? What are the furnishings?... (30 seconds) If there is anything which is not suitable, or to your taste, then change it... (1 minute) Create the colours you like best. Create the kind of seat you would find most comfortable... (1 minute) Are there flowers? Plants? Crystals? Paintings? Sculptures? A log fire? A fountain? Simply decide what you would like, and create it... (2 minutes) Make this sanctuary as comfortable, as cosy and as welcoming as possible... (1 minute) Adjust the temperature until it feels exactly right for you... (15 seconds) When you are ready, sit in your seat... (30 seconds) Know that this sanctuary is completely protected, completely safe... (30 seconds) Here, there is perfect peace, perfect tranquillity... (1 minute) You notice that directly in front of your seat, there is a screen... (30 seconds) This is your reality screen, and whatever you place upon the screen will be brought into reality in your day-to-day life... (30 seconds) When you are ready, begin to create, upon your screen, the reality you have chosen... (10 seconds) Whatever it is, picture the form and the detail... (10 seconds) The colours... (3 minutes) Now see yourself step into the reality you have created on the screen... (1 minute) How does it feel?... (1 minute) Picture your feelings... (10 seconds) Do you feel successful? Confident? Admired? Appreciated? Loved?... (10 seconds) See the you on the screen as you really want to be... (10 seconds) See everything happen as you really want it to happen... (10 seconds) Taste it... (10 seconds) Smell it... (10 seconds) Feel it... (5 minutes) Do you need to make any adjustments?... (1 minute) Add any details?... (1 minute) Step back from the screen and observe your creation... (3 minutes) This is your new reality. This is how things are going to be... (2 minutes) Now dissolve the image you have created on the screen... (30 seconds) Relax, knowing there is nothing further you need to do. Everything is taken care of and will happen, as you desire, when the time is right for you... (3 minutes) Now it is time to leave your sanctuary, knowing that this very special, very private place is always here for you... (1 minute) Take one last look around... (30 seconds) Leave by the door, making sure that you close the it behind you... (15 seconds) Step outside onto the moonlit path... (30 seconds) Retrace your steps back to the place where this inner journey began... (30 seconds) Prepare to enter your everyday life... (1 minute)

Close with chosen departure/grounding.

And finally, remember to...

Tread gently on the earth
Breathe gently of the air
Lie gently in the water
Touch gently to the fire

North American Chant

I am very keen to find out how you have applied the meditations in this book and also to learn about your experiences. As far as I am aware, to date there has been no serious research done on the effectiveness of guided meditation as a technique for healing and personal development.

I think it's time to let the scientists, the psychologists and the medical profession know that this way of working with mind, body and spirit really does produce results !

If you would like to take part in this project I would be very grateful if you could answer the questions which follow. If you would prefer to preserve your confidentiality, then there is no need to give your name, address or any other personal details. You may want to report on the results of just one guided meditation, or you may want to provide information relating to a number of inner journeys. Please feel free to send in as many questionnaires as you would like.

With love and light to everyone who reads this book, and my particular thanks to you if you decide to participate in the research project.

QUESTIONNAIRE

Name of the guided meditation:

Was there a particular reason why you chose to work with this meditation?

What happened for you as a result of working with this meditation? It would be very helpful if you could give specific examples of health, emotional or life changes.

> For example: Has there been a change in the physical or mental condition? Has a different or unexpected situation arisen? Has your way of dealing with circumstances related to this meditation, (e.g. relationships), changed in any way? Have you altered your direction in life?

Please send your responses to:
Lisa Davis
c/o Findhorn Press
The Press Building
The Park
Findhorn
Forres IV36 OTZ

Introducing Findhorn Press

Findhorn Press is the publishing business of the Findhorn Community which has grown around the Findhorn Foundation, co-founded in 1962 by Peter and Eileen Caddy and Dorothy Maclean. The first book originated from the early interest in Eileen's guidance over twenty years ago and Findhorn Press now publishes not only Eileen Caddy's books of guidance and inspirational material, but many other books, and it has also forged links with a number of like-minded authors and organisations.

For further information about the Findhorn Community and how to participate in its programmes please write to:

The Accommodation Secretary
Findhorn Foundation
Cluny Hill College, Forres IV36 0RD, Scotland
tel. +44(0)1309-673655 fax +44(0)1309-673113
e-mail reception@findhorn.org

For a complete catalogue, or for more information about Findhorn products, please contact:

Findhorn Press
The Park, Findhorn, Forres IV36 0TZ, Scotland
tel. +44(0)1309-690582 fax +44(0)1309-690036
e-mail thierry@findhorn.org

THE KINGDOM WITHIN   (£8.95) ISBN 905249 99 2
A Guide to the Spiritual Work of the Findhorn Community
Compiled and edited by Alex Walker

This collection of writings about the history, work, beliefs and practices of the Findhorn Foundation and its associated community of spiritual seekers offers a vision of hope, inspiration and encouragement. With contributions by David Spangler, William Bloom, Dorothy Maclean, Peter and Eileen Caddy amongst others, this book covers topics which include nature and ecology, the art of living in community, the relationship of 'new age' thought to formal religion, and co-operation with the spiritual worlds. The world is hungry for the hope and inspiration this brings—and so are you!

THE FINDHORN GARDEN   (£9.95) ISBN 0 905249 63 1
Pioneering a New Vision of Humanity and Nature in Cooperation
by The Findhorn Community

The story of the early days of the Findhorn Community and its communications with the nature kingdoms. Peter and Eileen Caddy's experiences as co-founders of the community, Dorothy MacLean's contact with the devas, R. Ogilvie Crombie's (ROC's) meetings with Pan and the Elemental Kingdom, and the wisdom of David Spangler and others combine to give a unique perspective on the relationship between humans and nature.

THE FINDHORN COMMUNITY (£8.95) ISBN 0 905249 771
by Carol Riddell

The author traces the community's development over the years and gives a clear picture of the community today and the new businesses and independent projects springing up around it. The second half of the book includes a number of intimate and revealing interviews with members, both young and old, who share their lives and experiences of living in this incredible community.

Guidebooks for Growth Together is a new collection of books launched by Findhorn Press in the spring of 1995. It consists of books addressed both to individuals and to groups who are looking for practical tools to help them on their siritual path.

Journeys Within is one of the first two books of the collection. Published simultaneously:

THE PATH TO LOVE IS THE PRACTICE OF LOVE
An Introduction to Spirituality, with Self-help Exercises for Small Groups   (£5.95) ISBN 1 899171 20 7
by Carol Riddell

This book explains the meaning of spiritual life, and provides a way for people to get together with like-minded friends to practice its principles. Through understanding and practice, there is the chance to transform daily life, or give meaning to its experiences and to find happiness in the service of others. The teachings can apply equally to Christians, Buddhists, Jews, Moslems, Hindus or Humanists, as long as it is accepted that the essential principle of the cosmos is love, a love both detached and personal, all-pervasive and specific. The exercises in this book have been tested out over a period of four years in workshops in several European countries and at the Findhorn Foundation. Several self-help groups have already used them as a basis.

There are more books in preparation for the autumn of 1995...